HOW TO CREATE THE CONDITIONS FOR LEARNING

Continuous Improvement in Classrooms, Schools, and Districts

ANN JAQUITH

Harvard Education Press
Cambridge, Massachusetts

Paperback ISBN 978-1-68253-082-5
Library Edition ISBN 978-1-68253-083-2

Library of Congress Cataloging-in-Publication Data
Names: Jaquith, Ann, author.
Title: How to create the conditions for learning : continuous improvement in
    classrooms, schools, and districts / Ann Jaquith.
Description: Cambridge, Massachusetts : Harvard Education Press, [2017]
Identifiers: LCCN 2017018612| ISBN 9781682530825 (pbk.) | ISBN 9781682530832
    (library edition)
Subjects: LCSH: Communities of practice—Case studies. | Professional
    learning communities—Case studies. | Educational leadership. |
    Instructional systems. | Teachers—In-service training--Case studies. |
    Teachers—Professional relationships—Case studies. | School
    superintendents--In-service training—Case studies.
Classification: LCC LB1707 .J35 2017 | DDC 371.2/011—dc23 LC record available
    at https://lccn.loc.gov/2017018612

Published by Harvard Education Press,
an imprint of the Harvard Education Publishing Group

Harvard Education Press
8 Story Street
Cambridge, MA 02138

Cover Design: Ciano Design
Cover Photo: FatCamera/Getty Images
The typefaces used in this book are ITC Stone Serif, ITC Stone Sans,
Museo Slab, and Museo Sans

For my mom and dad,
who were my first teachers.

For my husband,
whose love and encouragement
have made this book possible,
and for Jake and Zach,
who remind me daily of
what really matters.

CONTENTS

CREATING THE CONDITIONS FOR LEARNING

W hat does it take to create the conditions required to provide high-quality instruction every day to every student in our nation's classrooms? These conditions include knowing the strengths, interests, and needs of each student, having strong subject-area content knowledge, and knowing how to teach that content to individual students so they learn important concepts and disciplinary skills. They also include having the requisite instructional materials to support teaching and learning, knowing how to use those materials effectively, and having a workplace culture where educators are supported and expected to learn with and from each other so that they make sure all students learn to a high standard. I call this constellation of conditions *instructional capacity*. Exploring how to build such instructional capacity within a teacher team, among a school faculty, and within a school district is the subject of this book. Specifically, this book examines how to create the conditions for learning among three different groups of educators: teachers in schools, principals within a district, and a team of district administrators responsible for a group of schools.

PURPOSE OF THIS BOOK

The purpose of this book is to develop our conceptual and practical understanding of how to create the conditions for adult learning in schools and districts so that as educators we can do a better job of providing meaningful learning opportunities for all of our students. Many scholars have examined specific conditions that are needed to improve student learning. Some have focused on teachers and the qualities of excellent teaching; others have studied the role of the principal and the culture of the school; and still others have examined the role of the district office. Some research has called attention to the curriculum or to professional development; other studies have focused on professional community or the data-use practices of educators.

Each of these aspects of the educational milieu, as well as many others, contributes to creating conditions that are conducive to learning in schools. However, even though quite a bit has been written about what conditions are necessary for continuous instructional improvement, relatively little has been written about *how* to develop these conditions. One reason may be that the work entailed—such as creating organizational routines that help educators to collectively examine and adjust their practice—is complicated, messy, and not well understood. A contributing factor is the variability among districts and schools and the teams that work inside them. Because the workplace context affects and interacts with any change that is introduced into it—and no two educational settings are quite the same—there is no such thing as a foolproof recipe or prescribed steps for creating conditions that can ensure learning will occur.

One more complication is the inevitable interplay among various elements (i.e., teachers, administrators, students, curriculum, school culture, assessment practices, opportunities for collaboration, district expectations, and so on) that occurs when a change is introduced to a setting. Furthermore, the interplay may be hidden from view. Understanding the concept of instructional capacity can help elucidate this interplay and reveal the particular elements in the setting that are contributing to (or hindering) learning. Because these various elements are also often mutually influencing, it is difficult to know which action(s) to take, when, and under what conditions, as well as how to assess the effects of the actions taken. Given the complexity of creating the conditions for learning, I begin by offering a set of ideas and organizing principles about how to proceed. These ideas are linked together in a conceptual framework I call the instructional capacity building (ICB) framework.

FRAMING A WAY OF THINKING ABOUT HOW TO CREATE THESE CONDITIONS

First, a theory about the way a complex phenomenon works can be helpful. As Kurt Lewin famously remarked, "Nothing is quite so practical as a good theory."[1] I offer how to build instructional capacity as one such practical theory. This theory specifies what instructional capacity is and defines four types of instructional resources. As a concept, instructional capacity can be understood in terms of the instructional resources that are either available or can be generated in a particular context to achieve a particular learning goal as well as the knowledge needed to use these resources purposefully. Thus, instructional capacity is specific to each situation. The explication of instructional capacity, which I argue is a particular type of capacity, is useful since calls for "more capacity" have become commonplace in educational settings without really defining what this means. For instance, policy makers often bandy about the terms *capacity* and *capacity-building efforts* without precisely naming what is meant by capacity.

In addition to defining instructional capacity, this theory provides both a conceptual and a practical way to think about how to improve teaching and learning within schools, including which context features to pay attention to. The concepts that explain how instructional capacity is created provide us with handles to help us disentangle some of the complexity that exists in the nested learning environments in our schools and districts. The theory also describes in concrete terms what leaders can do to grow this capacity in the workplace.

HOW THIS BOOK IS ORGANIZED

This book has two main parts. The first (chapters 1 and 2) offers a conceptual discussion of instructional capacity and introduces the ICB framework, which provides a way to think about how to build this capacity. Chapter 1 introduces the concepts of instructional capacity and instructional resources. I define four types of instructional resources—instructional knowledge, instructional technology, instructional relationships, and organizational structures—and explain how each type is an asset for teaching and learning. I then discuss how the process by which instructional resources get identified and used in a particular context can promote or constrain the growth of instructional capacity. Chapter 2 describes how instructional resources get used in specific settings and to what effect. Here I also explain how using specific resources for a particular purpose can begin to generate additional instructional resources.

Part 2 (chapters 3–7) provides a close-up look at practice, using the ideas from the ICB framework to study several real-life examples of how educators try to create the conditions for learning in their workplace. Each chapter examines the use of instructional resources at a different level of the system and considers the various actions and practices that affect the growth of instructional capacity.

Chapter 3 describes the school-based conditions that affect whether teachers will use new instructional methods and tools in their teaching when provided with these tools. It also introduces the use of a handy conceptual tool that defines resource use along a spectrum. The specific examples of teachers, schools, and professional development programs described in chapters 3 and 4 are taken from a study I conducted to understand the conditions that enable professional development resources to get used by teachers. All names of people, places, and organizations in this book are pseudonyms, with the exception of the professional development program Reading Apprenticeship.[2]

Chapter 4 describes how instructional capacity grows by comparing two similar schools and examining the subtle, but significant, differences in leadership that led them to develop different levels of instructional capacity. At one school (Liberty Middle School), we see how the well-intentioned actions of a principal to accumulate resources for instructional improvement resulted in minimal creation of instructional capacity when the use of those resources was not given sufficient support. The story of the other school (Cedar Bridge Middle School) shows how instructional capacity grew through the intentional identification and use of instructional resources for the explicit purpose of strengthening the quality of student learning.

Chapter 5 focuses on how district supervisors can build principals' instructional leadership capacity and help them learn to lead instructional improvement. It tells the story of how a group of central office administrators in the Coopersville Union School District redesigned the purpose of principal meetings from simply communicating information to learning. The examples of principal and district leader learning experiences discussed in chapters 4–6 are drawn from various studies that I conducted in the Coopersville district over a period of five years.[3]

Chapter 6 discusses the new work that district administrators must undertake to support principal learning. It explores the various challenges that the team of district administrators confronted as they sought to reshape the form and function of district principal meetings. The conditions within the central office are described as are the sort of resources central offices need to have in order to increase instructional capacity district-wide.

Chapter 7 describes how researchers can help administrators expand their district's capacity for instructional leadership by facilitating opportunities for them to learn in and from their leadership work. I recount the role a research-practice partnership played in helping the Coopersville district team develop its instructional leadership capacity. (I led this research team.)

The concluding chapter ties the conceptual and practical discussions together and offers suggestions for what educators can do to develop instructional capacity across the entire system.

WHO SHOULD READ THIS BOOK?

This book is written for educators who are interested in improving the quality of learning—the learning opportunities that teachers provide for their students, that principals and school coaches provide for teachers, and that district administrators provide for principals as well as the learning opportunities that district leaders must provide for themselves.

Leaders who are responsible for instructional improvement at either the district or school level will find conceptual and practical ideas in this book that they can use. Specific examples taken from the field and viewed through the instructional capacity building framework help to answer questions like these:

- Under what conditions do instructional strategies introduced in professional development get taken up and used by teachers in their classrooms?
- What can principals do to improve the quality of teacher collaboration in their schools?
- How can district administrators help principals become more effective instructional leaders?

As an educator who has had many different roles (e.g., teacher, administrator, professional developer, school board member) and a researcher who has spent thousands of hours observing and working alongside those who are trying hard to offer high-quality instruction, I am sensitive to the various perspectives that can influence our understanding of how change is experienced as well as how we account for its various effects in the environment. The ICB framework helps illuminate the different dimensions of building instructional capacity and the various vantages from which to view a school's efforts to strengthen instruction and improve students' opportunities to learn. The examples offer specific guidance to educators within schools and in the central office about how to create the conditions for the meaningful use of instructional resources—which is the key to building instructional capacity.

PART I

"A PRACTICAL THEORY"

CHAPTER 1

THE INSTRUCTIONAL CAPACITY BUILDING FRAMEWORK

Knowledge, Technology, Organizational Structures, and Relationships

Instructional capacity comprises four types of instructional resources as well as the ability to use these resources to improve teaching and learning. Instructional improvement is what Bradley Portin and his colleagues refer to as the "substantial, observable shifts in teaching practice that enable students to be more successful."[1] A corollary to instructional improvement is the act of instructional leadership; these acts are the important, observable shifts in leadership practice that help teachers to make such changes to their practice. The instructional capacity building (ICB) framework offers a practical theory that explains how such shifts occur by illuminating the conditions under which instructional resources are identified, taken up, and generated. Knowing what instructional capacity is and how to expand it is essential for leading instructional improvement from any part of the educational system.

The ICB framework provides one way to understand when instructional resources get used and to make sense of the dynamic, interdependent, and complex processes of instructional improvement. For instructional resources to get taken up and used by individuals or groups, some sort of sense-making process must occur. The ICB framework draws on organizational and sociocultural learning theories to explain the conditions that enable or constrain the creation of instructional resources as well as the mechanisms for their identification and use.

Theories of organizational learning focus attention on the organization: its actions, structures, formal roles, and goals. An organizational perspective brings these features—the functional roles of organizational actors and units, the positional hierarchy and relative power of these individuals and groups—into the foreground. Sociocultural theories of learning view learning as a social process of participating in a joint enterprise[2] or in socially organized activities.[3] Sociocultural theories also emphasize the individual and collective sense making that occurs through participation. In this way, sociocultural theory lends itself to examining what occurs in the daily work of educators—for example, when they meet to plan curriculum, consider the effects of instruction on student learning, or attend professional development programs together.

Each theoretical perspective contributes to our understanding of how individuals and groups learn in community or group settings by illuminating different aspects of these settings.[4] Employing an organizational perspective allows us to examine the organizational dynamics at play that may promote or constrain the conditions necessary for the creation and use of resources for teaching. A sociocultural perspective—Etienne Wenger's theory of communities of practice, for instance—enables analysis of the social, relational, and cultural dynamics within and among various contexts.[5]

A brief vignette from a real school that I call Cedar Bridge follows.[6] This vignette explains the theoretical ideas that undergird instructional capacity and functions as a touchstone for the core ideas of this book, at once knitting together the practical and the conceptual. As you read this example, notice the conditions that support the learning that is going on.

CEDAR BRIDGE MIDDLE SCHOOL

At Cedar Bridge, the entire staff—teachers and administrators—gathered in the library on a Monday afternoon to work together in small groups. A poster of Richard DuFour's four essential questions for professional learning communities hung on the library wall:

- *What do we want students to learn?*
- *How will we know if students have learned it?*
- *What will we do if students don't learn?*
- *What will we do if they do?*

Nearby a sign offered this advice: "This work should be relevant and manageable."

The principal framed the work that teacher teams would engage in that afternoon: "We want to focus on nonsummative assessments to figure out exactly [what and] how our students are learning." Small groups of teachers, organized by grade level and subject area, were seated around rectangular tables with student work—essays, math problems, and science lab write-ups—spread out in front of them. Cedar Bridge's five school administrators were sprinkled among the teacher groups, but they were indistinguishable from the teachers who were reading student work and looking for evidence of understanding.

At this meeting, the sixth-grade humanities teachers worked together to assess the efficacy of a reading strategy—talking-to-the-text—that they used to teach the novel their sixth graders were reading—Christopher Paul Curtis's The Watsons Go to Birmingham—1963. *The teachers had been introduced to this strategy in a professional development program, and they were expected and supported to use this strategy in their instruction.*

Teachers read and discussed the sixth-grade samples of talking-to-the-text, which consisted of students' comments and questions written on sticky notes placed inside the pages of the novel. The administrator sitting with this team asked the teachers how they were using the talking-to-the-text strategy and what students' "text talk" revealed about their understanding. One teacher described how she used students' talk to focus class discussion and find out what confused her students. "During a confusing chapter," the teacher explained, "I had students keep the sticky notes in the book, and I looked through them . . . and picked out five common questions . . . which laid the foundation for the next class discussion."

For example, many students asked about Wool Pooh, a scary character invented by the narrator's brother to deter children from swimming in a dangerous place (Wool Pooh—think whirlpool). Other students wondered whether the main character—nine-year-old Kenny—believed in ghosts. Students' text talk also revealed that many students found the description of the bombing of the Birmingham church confusing. Teachers discovered that looking over the sticky notes was a useful way to see students' thinking—and doing so in order to plan for class discussion became a refined use of this strategy.

Other teachers suggested other approaches. One pointed out that she had students discuss their text-talk questions with one another in small groups. A first-year teacher in the group asked how the teachers helped students who struggled to "talk to the text." One colleague replied, "I have the students read aloud to me, and tell me their thoughts and questions. Then I prompt them to write those comments down."

Like all teacher groups in the library that afternoon, the sixth-grade humanities team analyzed students' work to develop a common lesson to teach in their classrooms that week. They also developed common criteria for assessing the student work that would result. Later in the same week, the teachers would look together at that new work to determine how well students had understood the lesson's focal concept or skill. Collectively, they would decide on their next instructional moves.

One instructional move they discussed was to have students make a list of how each character in the novel reacted to the church bombing. They also considered what they could do to help students become alert to the use of figurative language, which the novel is rich in. Another instructional move they debated concerned a chapter that most students found confusing. The teachers thought it might be a good idea to read that chapter out loud and then ask students to reread it to themselves and talk-to-the-text.

The teachers' common lesson plan grew out of these instructional conversations. This three-meeting cycle of developing common lessons rooted in teachers' collective examination of students' work occurred five times during the year.

CONDITIONS AND RESOURCES FOR
LEARNING AT CEDAR BRIDGE

What do you notice about the work the adults are doing together at Cedar Bridge? When I ask educators what stands out to them in this description, they usually make these sorts of observations: all the teachers were meeting in the library; they were organized by grade level and subject area; they were looking at samples of students' classroom work together; they were focused on considering four powerful questions about teaching and learning; and they were talking about how their students used a particular reading comprehension strategy, "talking-to-the-text." They notice that students had participated in a common grade-level assignment—reading *The Watsons Go to Birmingham*—and that students in all classrooms were using this reading strategy, which the teachers had learned during a professional development program. They observe that the administrators were participating in the teachers' examination of student work and exploring the teaching-learning relationship alongside the teachers. They also notice that the administrators blended in, were "indistinguishable" from the teachers, and did not appear to be in charge. They assume that there was trust among the teachers and between the teachers and the administrators. They assume that some degree of psychological safety existed such that the novice teacher could ask for help from her colleagues and receive it. They also see that the conversation centered on what teachers were noticing about their students as readers—how well their students understood this particular text, and how particular instructional moves affected students' understanding. Sometimes, they note that the teachers learned from each other, that they adapted their use of talking-to-the-text to the particular needs of individual students in their classrooms, and developed a new instructional purpose for this strategy. When educators read this vignette, they sense that this way of working was a familiar routine at Cedar Bridge.

Educators are often struck by this description of Cedar Bridge because it implies a way of adults working together in a school in which norms and practices that contribute to continuous improvement and meaningful collaboration are in place. A school environment is described where teachers are able to learn together, to ask questions of one another, and to help each other become better able to support students' learning in their classrooms. Educators often say that they would like their school to become more like Cedar Bridge. But making these observations about the description is just the first step; we also need to understand how to develop these sorts of conditions in our schools. A better understanding of how to help teachers focus on the relationship between their teaching and students' learning—and the conditions needed to do so—will help schools to grow their capacity for continuous instructional improvement.

WHAT IS INSTRUCTIONAL CAPACITY?

Broadly conceived, instructional capacity is the collection of resources for teaching that a district, school, or team has available to support instruction, and the ability to use these resources to teach in a manner that enables students to learn and be successful. I call them *instructional resources*.

In common language, resources are a supply, support, or aid that can be converted into assets. Resources also often refer to personal capabilities, such as expertise or interpersonal skills. In studies of education, resources for instruction are narrowly defined. Typically, they mean "money, curriculum materials and facilities."[7] These conceptions are usually restricted to physical resources, such as concrete materials like textbooks that are finite in number. When resources are treated as physical objects, four other presumptions have typically followed:

1. Resources are finite and get depleted.
2. Resources are located outside of the boundaries of the organization or subunit that requires the resource.
3. Access to resources is controlled by those with power.
4. Having access to a resource assumes its use—usually a uniform use.

These presumptions have significant and far-reaching implications for how districts, schools, and often teachers typically conceive of what instructional resources are, where to find them, and how to get them. Importantly, this mindset emphasizes the procurement of the resource rather than its use or creation. Since the common educational view of resources locates them outside of classrooms or schools, the need to accumulate resources permeates educational environments.

In the field of organizational studies, strategic management theorists define resources a bit more broadly as "the specific physical, human and organizational assets that can be used to implement value-creating strategies."[8] I extend and elaborate upon this definition, which Martha Feldman adopts in her study, "Resources in Emerging Structures and Processes of Change," to define a particular category of resources: instructional resources.[9]

Defining Instructional Resources

Instructional resources are particular assets that are used in the service of teaching and learning. Other sorts of important resources that do not directly pertain to instruction exist in schools too, such as school meal programs, family community centers, guidance counselors, and counseling programs. I classify four categories of instructional resources—knowledge, technology, organizational, and relational resources. All four categories of resources are needed to provide effective instruction to students:

1. Instructional technology (e.g., tools or materials such as curriculum, instructional tools, textbooks, teaching materials, assessments—and the know-how to use this technology effectively)
2. Instructional knowledge (including knowledge of content, pedagogy, and students)
3. Instructional relationships that are characterized by trust, mutual respect, recognition of instructional expertise, and openness to interpersonal learning
4. Organizational structures that support the identification, development, and use of instructional resources (e.g., common time for subject and/or grade-level teachers; formal instructional leadership roles and organizational mechanisms that foster teacher collaboration)

These four types of instructional resources are multifaceted and interdependent. Table 1.1 describes each type of instructional resource in more detail.

Instructional Technology Resources   Each profession has its own form of technology. The medical profession, for example, has various medical procedures and particular instruments for carrying out specific operations. The education profession also has its own forms of technology, one of which is

TABLE 1.1 *Four categories of instructional resources*

TECHNOLOGY RESOURCES	KNOWLEDGE RESOURCES	RELATIONAL RESOURCES	ORGANIZATIONAL RESOURCES
Methods (e.g., routines, frameworks, teaching strategies) *Tools* (e.g., devices) *Materials* (e.g., texts, curricula)	*Expertise in:* Content, pedagogy, pedagogical content knowledge, students and their backgrounds, local context	*Qualities of relation:* Trust, respect, integrity, psychological safety, recognition of another's specific expertise	*Structures* (e.g., staff, department, and grade-level meetings) *Formal roles* (e.g., leadership positions, coaches) *Practices and procedures* (e.g., organizational routines, norms for discussion)

instructional technology. Innovation scholars use the term technology to mean "a design for instrumental action that reduces the uncertainty in the cause-effect relationships involved in achieving a desired outcome."[10]

The same underlying aim guides the design of instructional technology—to reduce the uncertainty between teaching and learning. Instructional technology in the form of curricula, textbooks, teaching tools, instructional methods, and lesson plans is developed with the intention that it will increase the chances that learners will learn something in particular. For example, in the Cedar Bridge Middle School vignette, teachers use the instructional method of *talking-to-the-text*, which is intended to support active sense making while reading. The belief is that this particular strategy will increase the likelihood that students are able to make meaning while they are reading and to talk about or recall that meaning.

The term *instructional technology* embodies two components: (1) a *hardware* aspect, consisting of the tool that embodies the technology as a material or physical object, and (2) a *software* aspect, consisting of the information base for the tool.[11]

Both hardware and software aspects of instructional technology are important. The software aspect, however, is often not given much consideration by the procurer or its user.

Hardware aspects of instructional technology include instructional materials (e.g., texts, curricula, maps, problem sets, and comprehension questions) and raw materials (e.g., dice, popsicle sticks, and sticky notes) that in their use are transformed into tools. Consider the transformation of sticky notes into repositories for "text talk" or of popsicle sticks into "Equity Sticks" when used to select students for a task instead of calling upon students who raise their hands. We commonly think of tools for teaching as instructional technology. These tools or devices may be an articulation of an instructional method (e.g., a curriculum, script, discussion protocol, or conceptual framework), or they may provide support for enacting a method (e.g., a binder of professional development materials, a teacher's manual, a codified list of steps, or an assessment).

Instructional technology also has a software aspect that provides the informational base for the tool. Instructional technology software encompasses information or data as well as the instructional methods, approach, and educational philosophy. Such software does not always have accompanying hardware. For instance, talking-to-the-text, a reading routine that helps readers make their thinking-while-reading visible, does not have accompanying tools like worksheets or a codified list of explicit steps to follow. When the software of instructional technology does have associated hardware, there is often an intended relationship between the instructional tool and its specified use. Scripted curricula provide an extreme case of how instructional tools sometimes rigidly specify the enactment of a particular instructional method. Here, the software and hardware of instructional technology are tightly coupled by design. This tight coupling also conveys a particular perspective about the role of the teacher in providing instruction.

Both the hardware and software aspects of an instructional technology are embodied in a lesson plan, for example. The written plan constitutes the concrete tool (particularly useful, for instance, when conveying the lesson plan to a substitute teacher). The software aspect of the plan might include the lesson's purpose and instructional methods, which are often tacit. The extent to which the enacted lesson diverges from the written plan illuminates the relationship that exists between the software and hardware of this instructional technology; the relationship can be understood as having a tight or loose connection.

Because the software aspect of instructional technology is often not visible, we tend to think of instructional technology in hardware terms. Indeed, we're apt to assume that having the hardware aspect of instructional technology is sufficient—we presume that having it means using it. For example, if a teacher is given a lesson plan, then the assumption is that he/she can teach the lesson. Anyone who has tried to follow a lesson plan, however, knows that a lesson plan usually does not convey all the information needed to teach the lesson well.

Assessments are another example of instructional technology that has both hardware and software aspects and demonstrates how the software aspects can be overlooked. We typically think of assessments as hardware, the physical object (the actual test), and pay less attention to its software aspects—the information base used for designing a particular assessment. But the information is important. It is what influences the selection and sequencing of the assessment's content and the design of individual questions. Understanding the software aspects of an assessment can influence performance. This is why a test preparation industry has emerged that explicitly teaches the "software aspects" of high-stakes standardized tests to future test takers for a fee. The software aspect of an assessment also provides the information from which to discern what that particular measure of learning values.

As described earlier, one instructional technology used at Cedar Bridge Middle School was talking-to-the-text, a teaching method to help readers actively make sense of what they are reading. This instructional technology does not really have a hardware component, although the students' sticky notes—where readers jot down their ideas and questions about the text while they read—are the physical manifestation of the talking-to-the-text strategy in use. The information base that comprises the "software" of this tool—what to write down on the sticky notes while reading—is not visible. The purpose of this instructional method is to provide a way for students to make their thinking while reading visible and explicit to themselves and to others. Readers' thinking ordinarily remains hidden. Thus, the act of writing down one's thinking, not the physical object of the sticky note, is what constitutes the essence of this particular instructional technology.[12]

Knowledge Resources This instructional resource refers to a person or group with knowledge needed for meaningful instruction. This knowledge may be static (knowledge of subject-area content) or performance-based (how to teach specific subject-area concepts to particular students). I distinguish four types of knowledge that are particularly relevant for instruction: knowledge of subject matter (i.e., content knowledge and pedagogical content knowledge; in the Cedar Bridge example this included knowledge of literature and literary devices and of teaching reading comprehension skills); knowledge of pedagogy (including classroom management and the organization of differentiated and individualized support to students); knowledge of the individual learner (including background, culture, and language) as well as knowledge of the group context; and knowledge of particular instructional technology relevant to the learning goals (such as the curriculum and assessments).[13] In the Cedar Bridge example, the instructional method of talking-to-the-text became essential knowledge for all teachers to possess because of the school's shared commitment to using this particular technology.

Knowing about a particular instructional technology that is relevant for the teaching of specific subject matter to specific students may or may not include *knowledge of how to use those resources in that setting.* Knowing how to use particular instructional resources is a distinct type of knowledge that often gets acquired through the use of the technology. For example, at Cedar Bridge we see the sixth-grade humanities teachers learning how to use talking-to-the-text to identify individual and collective student confusion about the text, to guide their selection of focal questions for subsequent class discussions, and to create customized instructional supports for individual students who don't know how to describe their thinking as they read a piece of literature. Because this knowledge is acquired when the technology is used, supporting meaningful use of instructional technology is an important strategy for building instructional capacity. (This strategy is explored in chapter 3).

Organizational Resources This resource refers to structural assets that benefit instruction within an organization (e.g., allocation of time for instructional meetings at the grade-level, department, or school levels, such as the professional learning community meetings that occurred in the Cedar Bridge library) and the designation of formal roles and responsibilities (e.g., of administrators or formal teacher leaders). Of particular interest is how these formal leadership roles are structured and enacted for instructional purposes, such as administrators' participation in the Cedar Bridge professional learning community conversations. Organizational resources for instruction also include the routines and practices that exist within an organization to support instruction (e.g., a school's process for selecting professional development programs and then following up on their implementation in classrooms, as was done at Cedar Bridge). These organizational routines and practices convey the way things are done in a school or department as well as what is valued. Moreover, such practices communicate the organization's beliefs about leaders and teachers as learners and decision makers. These enacted routines are a manifestation of an organization's culture or subculture.[14] The practices and norms of everyday actions reveal the tacit knowledge held and conveyed by organizational actors—both individual and collective.

For the purposes of understanding how to grow instructional capacity, the leadership structure of the school—often embodied by the school principal and a team of other administrators and/or formal teacher leaders—also needs to be viewed as an organizational resource that influences the types of instructional resources that a school has, as well as how these resources are used.[15] Schools have various leadership structures and styles.[16] Increasingly, the role of the school leader in developing the organizational capacity of the school to continuously improve teaching and learning is receiving more attention in the research literature.[17] As many leadership scholars suggest, the beliefs and actions of the leader at the helm of the organization will affect the sort of instructional resources—particularly organizational and relational resources—that are readily accessible to individuals and groups within the organization.

In Cedar Bridge, many organizational structures were used specifically to support ongoing instructional improvement. For example, the cycle of teacher collaboration meetings was an organizational structure that Cedar Bridge created in order to focus teacher attention on examining the relationship between evidence of student learning and the instruction they received. Cedar Bridge created a leadership team that functioned as a sort of teacher collaboration task force for the purpose of planning for and overseeing the design, facilitation, and degree of teacher learning that occurred during these meetings.

Relational Resources   This fourth instructional resource refers to interpersonal relationships and the quality of those relationships (e.g., trust and respect) as well as the perception of individual instructional expertise (e.g., perceived pedagogical or instructional resource knowledge). Within a school community people form relationships with one another for a variety of reasons, including friendship. To better understand what instructional capacity is, I want to highlight the particular kind of relationship that forms among educators when matters pertaining to instructional practice and evidence of student learning are central. These instructionally focused relationships seem to require the perception and attribution of instructional expertise on the part of at least one individual in the relationship. Two other elements of these relationships are also evident and help distinguish colleagues who act as instructional relational resources for one another (as opposed to those who, by their organizational position, are simply grade-level or departmental colleagues, for example). These two elements are the strength of the relational tie and the degree of relational trust that exists between people. The strength of relational ties, as it pertains to perceived instructional expertise, can be measured in part by the frequency with which teachers and administrators seek out a particular individual regarding instruction and student learning.

Tony Bryk and Barbara Schneider offer a helpful conception of relational trust, which is an important component in any relationship.[18] They determined that *relational trust* is "key to advancing improvement in urban public school communities" and point out that in the context of school reform, trust is particularly important because "organizational change entails major risks for all participants."[19] Their argument that relational trust is a core resource for school improvement is useful for our purposes. The decision to adopt a particular instructional approach or resource requires some change for the user (such as a teacher or principal) and, therefore, invariably involves risk.

Bryk and colleagues developed four criteria for discerning relational trust: respect, competence, personal regard for others, and integrity. These criteria help to determine the extent of relational trust that exists between individual teachers within a single school and between teachers and the principal or leadership team. Relational trust is an important element of social relations and affects how individuals get along and work together in groups. Furthermore, it is not fixed. Rather, relational trust grows or wanes depending upon various conditions and actions.

Bryk and colleagues "posit a dynamic interplay" among respect, competence, personal regard for others, and integrity and suggest that "a serious deficiency on any one criterion can be sufficient to undermine a discernment of trust for the overall relationship."[20] Among the team of sixth-grade teachers at Cedar Bridge, we can infer a relatively high level of relational trust given that the teachers bring samples of their students' work to the meetings for their colleagues to examine and that teachers are comfortable seeking out help from one another when struggling to effectively use the talking-to-the-text instructional strategy. When the first-year teacher asks for help and receives a useful suggestion from her colleague, we can infer that such interactions are likely to increase the teacher's sense of personal regard for her colleague and attribute competence to her. In a study of seventy-eight elementary schools in eight districts, Susan Rosenholtz found that help-giving behaviors among teachers are reported in school environments where teaching is viewed as complex and where teachers are encouraged to collaborate with each other to develop effective teaching strategies.[21] In schools with these characteristics, relationships focused on instruction seem more likely to exist.

Becoming a Resource for Teaching Implies Its Use

These four types of instructional assets become *resources for teaching and learning* when they are put to some sort of use. Moreover, their use may generate other instructional resources in the form of actions, ideas, tools, or instructional relationships. In addition, effective use of one type of instructional resource often involves using the other types of instructional resources. For example, to use the talking-to-the-text strategy in a meaningful way, teachers must have or must develop knowledge of subject matter, of literary devices, and of their students. If a school, like Cedar Bridge, wishes to have its teachers develop their knowledge of how to use this instructional method to strengthen students' reading skills, then organized opportunities are also needed for teachers to work together to figure out how to implement talking-to-the-text in their classrooms. Through these opportunities, teachers try out, discuss, and deliberate aspects of teaching and learning with each other—thereby increasing their capacity for developing instructional relationships. Indicators that instructional resources are being used might include changes in educators' thoughts, relationships, and practices as well as the development of organizational structures and routines.

CREATING RESOURCES: THE INSTRUCTIONAL RESOURCING CYCLE

The *instructional resourcing cycle* is a process that explains how instructional resources get generated in practice. The concept of resourcing comes from organizational scholar Martha Feldman.[22] During her study of a university human resource department, she developed this construct, which she defines as "the creation *in practice* of assets such as people, time, money, knowledge or skill; and qualities of relationships such as trust, authority, or complementarity such that they enable actors to enact schemas."[23] Feldman suggests assets are created as work is carried out, through actions; they are recognized as potential resources because of people's ideas and beliefs about how things work (their schema) and are put to use in the actions that people take, which derive from people's ideas and beliefs. Feldman's key idea is that these resources or assets are created *in practice*. Resources are not static nor are they located entirely outside, or necessarily within, an organization. Rather, resources are generated in action.

Explaining the Relationships Among the Resourcing Elements

I build upon Feldman's conception by developing an instructional resourcing cycle that is bidirectional and recursive, in which instructional resources (assets), schema, and actions influence one another (see figure 1.1). In other words, actions as well as beliefs mediate the use of assets—actions also influence beliefs—transforming assets into instructional resources through their specific use. My use of Feldman's resourcing construct is not only to show how resources for instruction are generated

FIGURE 1.1 *The instructional resourcing cycle*

in various contexts, but also to illuminate how resources get identified, understood, and used by educators at different levels of the system in order to improve teaching and learning. Some educational researchers have argued that new ideas or understanding lead to new actions, and, conversely, others have argued that new actions lead to new understanding.[24] Recognizing the interrelationship between ideas and actions, I have modified Feldman's resourcing cycle by inserting bidirectional arrows (figure 1.1). As researchers have cautioned, it is difficult to change an individual's ideas, and it is perhaps more difficult to accurately detect a change in an individual's ideas because "apparent inconsistencies and counterexamples often are easily assimilated into the schemata to which a person is committed."[25] In other words, people often are not persuaded by evidence or examples to change their beliefs. Misconceptions endure.[26]

In the Cedar Bridge example, we see that the school leaders' schema about how learning occurs and about the role of administrators led them to participate in the teachers' subject-area conversations, but not to direct these conversations or micromanage them. Initially, Cedar Bridge leaders wanted teachers to examine standardized test score data to figure out how to support the lowest performing students, but teachers had different schema about which student data would be most useful for discovering what students were learning and what adjustments they needed to make to their instruction.[27] And, according to Cedar Bridge teachers' schema, standardized test scores were not terribly helpful in this regard.

The teachers' schema, informed by their past experiences, rejected the principal's initial focus on standardized test scores as a guide for immediate instructional decision making. They did not consider examining this data to be a meaningful activity. Some teachers were quite insistent that standardized test score data gathered months ago was not useful if the goal was to inform instructional decisions that they would need to make tomorrow and next week. Teachers explained they were now teaching different content. Thus, teachers' schema pointed to students' classroom work as more meaningful student performance data. Because the principal and other school leaders valued teachers' knowledge, they listened to teachers' concerns. The more the leaders listened to teachers on staff—especially those they regarded highly—the more they realized the truth in what the teachers were saying. Consequently, the leaders decided to change the focus of teachers' collaborative conversations; they directed teachers to select samples of students' classroom work to look at together. In so doing, the principal and other formal leaders demonstrated their capacity to alter their own thinking (their schema) and, importantly, modeled a learning stance.

Community of Practice as a Place Where Instructional Resources Get Created

The instructional resourcing cycle provides a way to view or understand practices associated with instructional resources—their identification, use, and creation. According to Wenger, participation in a practice always involves a duality of participating in as well as giving form to that experience.[28] The collective learning that results from a shared endeavor, Wenger says, "results in practices that reflect both the pursuit of our enterprises and the attendant social relations."[29] Wenger calls the community that results from a sustained joint enterprise a *community of practice.*

In the conversation that occurred among the sixth-grade humanities teachers at Cedar Bridge, we see that teachers were engaged in a sustained joint enterprise of looking together at students' common formative assessments over time. From the vignette, we can discern that these teachers were developing their own community of practice. As sociocultural theorists suggest, it is also critical to recognize the context where this learning is occurring, as this can be helpful for understanding the interplay between the context and the instructional resources—their identification, use, and creation.[30]

LOCATING THE INSTRUCTIONAL RESOURCING CYCLE IN A CONTEXT

In the field of education, the learning process is frequently depicted as consisting of three components: student, teacher, and content. These three components are typically represented in a triangular relationship wherein the interaction between them is the locus of learning.[31] I recast this locus of learning as the context in which resource use is situated and suggest four context dimensions that affect the use and creation of instructional resources—purpose (*why*), participants (*who*), content (*what*), and structure (*how*). See figure 1.2.

Schools afford multiple contexts in which instructional resources are identified and put to some use. Professional development programs also provide a context in which instructional resources are made available and often put to use. Sometimes these contexts are nested—such as grade-level teams (e.g., eighth-grade teachers) that belong to a particular department (e.g., English Department). Sometimes these contexts overlap (a cohort

FIGURE 1.2   *The four context dimensions that influence learning*

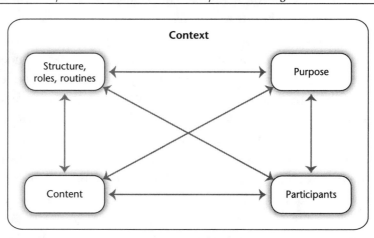

of teachers from one school might participate in a professional development network outside of school). Other times, contexts where resources get used exist in relative isolation. Whatever the configuration of these contexts, their location within the organization and their relationship to one another matters for the identification, use, and movement of instructional resources.

These four context dimensions are interrelated in complex and dynamic ways, as the figure illustrates. The two-way arrows connecting these four dimensions represent their interplay. For instance, we can imagine that a teacher's instructional purpose will influence the content she selects and how she approaches her instruction. We can also imagine that each of these instructional decisions will be made with particular students in mind. In other words, a teacher who has one classroom of English language learners and another of Advanced Placement English students will probably select different content and structure her lesson differently even if her instructional purpose for both lessons is essentially the same. Of course, teachers and professional developers (including administrators or teachers leading on-site workshops) do not always consider these four context dimensions (or are not always able to attend to them) as they plan and enact their instruction. This is a common problem of professional development practice.

The Re-creation or Transformation of Resources

In her theory of resourcing, Feldman sets out to describe the process by which resources are generated in action.[32] Although Feldman conceives of resourcing as occurring in practice, she does not explicitly consider the sociocultural dimensions of how resources are created or how the particular context might influence the resourcing process. For instance, her theory does not attend to the social context in which resourcing occurs. Nor does she explicitly consider how participants in a practice are connected or how they influence one another. In short, her study does not explore how resourcing occurs within the context of joint activity. In schools, joint activity is likely to occur in team meetings when adults are engaged in a shared enterprise, such as looking at student work to guide instructional decisions (as in the Cedar Bridge teacher team meetings), and within classrooms when students become a community of learners rather than individual learners. (See the description of Will's classroom in chapter 3.)

Feldman's practice-based theory of organizational resourcing does offer a different and more dynamic way for educators and organizational theorists to think about the location and origin of resources for instruction. She shows how "changes in the internal processes of an organization can take one kind of resource and recreate it as a different resource."[33] In the context of schools, changes to internal processes can also take one kind of resource and recreate it as a different resource, as the following example of Cedar Bridge illustrates.

Often when teachers meet in grade-level or course teams, they are expected to submit notes from their meeting to the principal. The purpose of submitting these notes is essentially to document that the meeting occurred and what was discussed. This activity is typically treated in a perfunctory manner by teachers and viewed as an activity with which they must comply. However, changes to the internal processes at Cedar Bridge led to a new idea and purpose for these "mandatory notes." This different conception of their use transformed meeting notes into a different type of resource. For instance, at Cedar Bridge, teacher teams were expected to submit notes after their first professional learning cycle meeting, but the purpose of the notes was to document teachers' insights and planned actions. The form and structure of the notes reflected this learning purpose. Teachers were asked to respond to questions such as "What were the results of the formative assessment you gave?"; "What specific difficulties did students have with the material they were supposed to learn?"; "Which students/how many had those difficulties?"; and "What specific instructional strategies are you going to use to address the learning of those students who had difficulty?" Furthermore, because the Cedar Bridge leadership team gave the teachers feedback on their notes at their next meeting, notes that formerly might have served a compliance purpose now served a learning purpose for the teachers and for the administrative leaders.

In this example, the identification of a resource for a particular use not only "recreates it as a different resource," in Feldman's terms, but also connects the identification (or re-creation) of the resource to a particular need or problem. At Cedar Bridge the leaders wanted a way to focus teachers' conversations on examining the relationship between teaching and student learning as well as a way to support teachers in this new professional practice. In this example, we see the process of selecting a resource (documentation of a meeting) and determining which actions to take so that the specific use of the resource matches the learning purpose and addresses the users' learning needs. In so doing, the resourcing cycle (the relationship among the actor's schema, actions, and resources) is tightly connected to the learning context (its purpose, participants, content, and activity structure). The selection and design of this particular resource (the meeting notes) helped structure the activity within the teachers' professional learning community meetings. Thus through the lens of instructional capacity building, at Cedar Bridge we can see a reciprocal relationship between the four context dimensions and the resourcing cycle.

The Nature of Resource Identification and Its Relationship to Context

The identification of instructional resources shapes and is shaped by the learning environment and actors' beliefs. This idea is not new. Scholars, who research the spread of ideas, have long studied how adopters' perceptions of an innovation, such as its relative advantage or compatibility, affect the rate of adoption.[34] Sense-making theorists also describe how actors make sense of situations that are puzzling or uncertain—and, in order to do so, "select what [they] will treat as the 'things' of the situation."[35] In the example of the Cedar Bridge meeting notes, the "things" of the situation were the teachers' conceptions of the learning difficulties that particular students demonstrated. Wenger describes this sense-making process as a "negotiation of meaning."[36] He proposes that an interesting question to ask in any negotiation of meaning is "how the production of meaning is distributed, that is, what is reified and what is left to participation."[37] The process of identifying resources as well as re-creating or inventing them, then, can be understood as part of the sense-making process. To this point, Karl Weick refers to Donald Schon's discussion of problem setting to conclude: "Problem setting is a process in which, interactively, we name the things to which we will attend and frame the context in which we will attend to them."[38] Knowing the particular context is, therefore, critical for understanding how problems are selected and how meanings are negotiated.

Empirical Evidence Shows a Relationship Between the Context and Instructional Resources

In education over the past decade, scholars have provided evidence that the context in which teachers work also shapes and influences what and how they learn.[39] For instance, scholarship on reforming school districts has paid increasing attention to the district as a context that identifies and disseminates instructional resources to schools.[40] Together, these studies illuminate ways in which the district and school contexts influence how schools, grade-level teams, and individual teachers take up and implement a reform. Mary Kay Stein and Cynthia Coburn conceptualize district reforms as the "'stuff' that embodies [the district's] vision (e.g., curricular frameworks, directives, or procedures)" and conceive of the district's role as seeking "to identify or create 'stuff.'"[41] Stein and Coburn argue that the "stuff" (the instructional resources) that a district identifies affects the learning opportunities that are created for teachers.[42] For example, in their study of two different school districts that adopted different mathematics curricula, they find that the features of the two curriculum materials (i.e., instructional technology) afforded teachers different opportunities "to apprehend the purpose of the activities."[43] The theory of instructional capacity building goes further and suggests that not only does the identified stuff affect the learning opportunities, but the manner in which the stuff is identified, introduced to teachers (or other users), and how the teachers are supported to use it affects the opportunities for learning that are created.

Stein and Coburn also show how mechanisms that connect professional communities at various levels within the system "mediate teachers' opportunities to learn in response to district policy."[44] Add to this the idea that individuals and groups experience these organizational contexts and their connecting mechanisms differently, as scholars who study organizational culture have shown, and it becomes clear that various individual and collective school actors—teachers, teams of teachers, and the school—will have different perceptions of what an instructional resource is.[45] Individual decisions about whether or not to use the identified resource will differ. Which things or practices actors identify as instructional resources will also vary by person, time, and place. Use of resources will vary too. Similarly, an instructional resource identified by one person might get dismissed by this same person in another circumstance, and be overlooked in a third situation. Therefore, focusing attention on the identification of instructional resources is important because it connects instructional resources to particular perceived problems or needs.

CHAPTER 2

THE INSTRUCTIONAL RESOURCING CYCLE
Identification, Use, Creation, and Transfer

This chapter explores the conditions that enable a meaningful use of instructional resources as well as conditions that lead to a more mechanical or contrived use of instructional resources. This chapter shows how, through the purposeful use of instructional resources, other instructional resources get created. This pattern of instructional resourcing occurs when the use of the resource is connected to the particular learning dimensions or needs of a context. This occurrence is described as fitting the resource to the context.

SITUATING THE INSTRUCTIONAL RESOURCING CYCLE WITHIN A CONTEXT

Instructional resourcing occurs within a context, as depicted in figure 2.1. The context matters and influences the use of the resource and the extent of learning that occurs.

The two-way arrows flowing in and away from the instructional resourcing cycle are meant to depict the process of *fitting* the instructional resource to the context. These arrows show that the creation and use of instructional resources is affected by, and in turn will affect to varying degrees, the four dimensions of the learning context. Through the process of fitting we can conceive of different types of resource use. For instance, not all users of the same instructional resource will use that resource in the same manner or for precisely the same purpose. For example, the meeting

FIGURE 2.1 *Fitting the instructional resourcing cycle within a context*

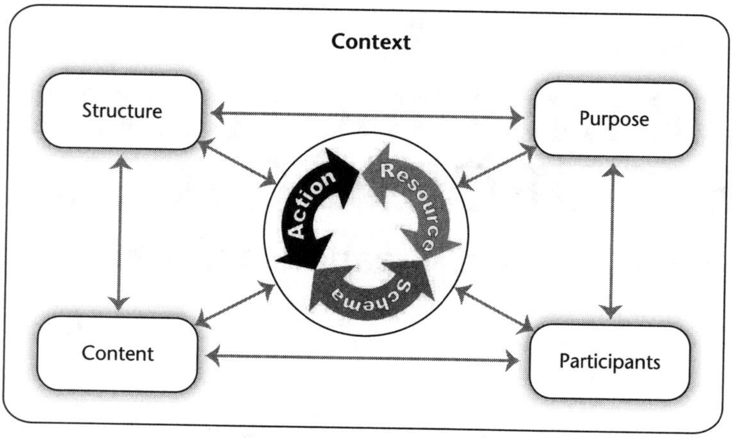

note template at Cedar Bridge was not used in exactly the same way by each grade-level and subject-area team. Therefore, I propose a typology that distinguishes three types of resource use: adoption of the resource, adaptation of the resource, and transformation or invention of a resource. I define these three types of resource use this way:

- *Adoption* marks what is often the initial use of an identified resource. It is characterized by using a resource "with fidelity" and without fitting its use to the particular context. Adoptive use is evident when a user goes through the motions of using the resource but lacks a complete understanding of the resource's purpose or how to use it to achieve that purpose.
- *Adaptation* refers to the process of fitting the instructional resource to the particular context dimensions and the specific learning purpose. A telling characteristic of adaptation is making adjustments to the resource (or perhaps to the context) so that its use better serves the user's learning purpose and the participants' needs.
- *Transformation* is distinguishable from adaptation when such significant changes or alterations are made to the instructional resource that it is said to be re-created, or if a new use/purpose for the resource is developed.

In addition, instructional resources get created through the fitting process.

Resource creation—such as developing an instructional tool or method or designing new organizational structures or formal roles to support teaching and learning—typically occurs when existing instructional resources (and their current use) are not sufficient to achieve a learning purpose or to respond to an identified learning need. For example, at Cedar Bridge, professional learning community meetings were a new form of meeting created so teachers could examine student work together, learn the practice of connecting their teaching to evidence of student learning, and hone their use of particular instructional strategies, like talking-to-the-text. These meetings represented a new organizational structure (an instructional organizational resource) at Cedar Bridge. This meeting structure was created when school leaders realized teachers thought the predominant purpose of their team meeting time was to plan lessons rather than to examine student work. School leaders wanted to shift teachers' focus away from merely planning lessons to looking at what students were doing and producing. They wanted teachers to consider if, and to what extent, students were actually learning particular skills and concepts.

FITTING AN INSTRUCTIONAL RESOURCE TO A CONTEXT GENERATES INSTRUCTIONAL RESOURCES

The process of fitting a resource to a particular context initiates its use, which is often an adaptive use. For instance, almost as soon as the administrators at Cedar Bridge began to use the meeting note template, they discovered that some teachers planned to help students who did not understand concepts by teaching the content again in the same manner. The Cedar Bridge administrators wanted teachers to develop and try different strategies rather than to repeat the approach that had not yet worked. Thus, the Cedar Bridge leaders decided it would further their overall learning goal for teachers if they looked at each team's meeting notes and provided specific feedback to the teacher teams. This example shows Cedar Bridge administrators *fitting* their use of the meeting note template to cohere with their original purpose for the professional learning community meetings and trying to figure out how to meet the particular learning needs of the Cedar Bridge teachers that they identified. In the next section

I describe a tool that can help us understand what is required for the fitting process to succeed.

THE SPECTRUM OF INSTRUCTIONAL RESOURCE USE

Viewing the use of an instructional resource along two dimensions—clarity of the learning goal and knowledge of learners—helps us discern the effectiveness of using a specific resource in that particular setting. The *resource use spectrum* tool, shown in figure 2.2, prompts several questions:

- What learning do I want the use of this resource to achieve?
- What do I need to do to make it more likely that using this particular resource with these learners will achieve the learning goal?
- How will I know if use of the resource is effective?

The resource use spectrum illuminates the importance of having well-specified instructional goals and knowledge of the learners. It calls attention to two dimensions of the learning context: the purpose and the participants. The other two dimensions of the context that matter for learning—the content and the activity structure—are embedded in the resource selection and its particular use.

FIGURE 2.2 *Resource Use Spectrum*

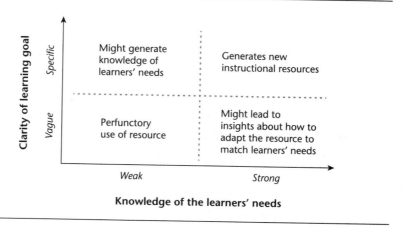

The Cedar Bridge example shows that through the fitting process, the resource user (in this instance, the administrators) negotiated a meaningful and purposeful use of the resource (to help teachers refine and develop instructional strategies aimed specifically at students who did not understand the initial explanation). The administrators simultaneously created the conditions to sustain its use within the context of the professional learning community meetings. One condition they created to sustain the use of the meeting notes, which were intended to help teachers to adjust their instructional practice, was the provision of specific and timely feedback on the notes.

The fitting process also plays a critical role in generating instructional resources for use, as the spectrum of resource use outlines. In the Cedar Bridge example, we might describe the administrators' debriefing meetings to look at the teacher teams' notes, as well as the new practice of providing teachers with written feedback, as instances of instructional resource creation. The use of these resources may in turn have also led to stronger and deeper instructional relationships between some of the Cedar Bridge administrators and teachers.

In the Cedar Bridge vignette, we can also notice that the sixth-grade teachers put the talking-to-the-text strategy into use in their classrooms in such a way that their use of this strategy was *fitted* to students' learning needs, which, in turn, led the teachers to invent new ways to use talking-to-the-text. Once the strategy was being used purposefully, the teachers recognized that reading across students' text talk could help them identify areas in the text that the students found challenging to understand. This use revealed a new purpose for talking-to-the-text: lesson planning. Teachers discovered that learning what students were thinking at various points in the text provided them with useful information for planning their subsequent lessons. In this way, examining the use of talking-to-the-text across the sixth-grade humanities team involved both using this instructional method and simultaneously getting new ideas for how to use it.[1] By fitting the use of this instructional resource to the classroom context, in particular their students' learning needs, the teachers adapted their use of talking-to-the-text and refined their use of the strategy. (For further discussion, see chapter 3.)

SOCIOCULTURAL FEATURES AFFECT THE USE OF INSTRUCTIONAL RESOURCES

The structural and sociocultural features of the setting interact in dynamic ways with the use of a particular instructional resource. Individual and collective beliefs and actions affect the particular way in which an instructional resource gets used. Wenger theorizes about the complementarity of this relationship:

> The complementarity of participation and reification yields an obvious but profound principle for endeavors that rely on some degree of continuity of meaning—communication, design, instruction, or collaboration. Participation and reification must be in such proportion and relation as to compensate for their respective shortcomings. When too much reliance is placed on one at the expense of the other, the continuity of meaning is likely to become problematic in practice.[2]

We see this balance of participation and reification (i.e., making an abstract idea more concrete) as teachers figured out how to use the talking-to-the-text strategy in their own classrooms. Teachers were actively using the strategy (participating in its use) and figuring out simultaneously how to reify it—to design an approach or way to use it that was meaningful. Cedar Bridge teachers worked together to develop a common approach, so that they could use the talking-to-the-text strategy to strengthen their teaching in ways that would help all of their students to articulate their thinking about what they read. We see the "complementarity of participation and reification" in action when the teachers discussed how to make this method work for students who were unable, for whatever reason, to write down their thinking while reading. Teachers reified their use of talking-to-the-text by telling each other stories about how they were using this method in their classrooms with various students. By telling these stories, teachers developed collective practices for using the strategy. Thus, the process of fitting an instructional resource into the context in which it is used can help preserve or create meaning through its fitted use. The importance of participating in the use of an instructional resource in order to develop one's understanding of that resource signals problems that are inherent in the movement of instructional resources from one location to another.

THE CREATION AND MOVEMENT OF INSTRUCTIONAL RESOURCES

The instructional capacity building framework (figure 2.3) shows several settings in which instructional resourcing occurs within schools and at the intersection of schools and an external professional development provider. The latter could be the central office, which also sits outside of the school context, or it could be another organization, external to the district. (Chapters 3 and 4 consider examples of professional development provided by an external professional development provider, and chapters 5 and 6 look at examples of district-led professional development.) When trying to understand if, or how, an instructional resource is getting used, it is always important to consider the origin of the resource, as well as the intent and design (the "software" elements) and the "hardware" elements. Equally significant is how the resource came to the learning context, which is often a school: by what means and along what pathways did the instructional resource travel? As researchers have pointed out, physical resources themselves do not carry the capacity for learning.[3] Moreover, an instructional resource itself does not cause learning to occur. For learning to occur, the resource must get used, and this use always happens within a particular setting.

The instructional capacity building framework offers a conceptual lens for looking at the relationship between the various contexts where professional learning is intended to occur. The framework identifies three specific contexts—the external professional development context and two within-school contexts, the professional community and the classroom—as likely places in which the processes of instructional resourcing and fitting take place. The framework provides a way to understand the generation of resources and their use at the intersection of two contexts where professional learning is intended to occur. The framework also offers a conceptual map that shows three different, but related, contexts where the instructional resourcing cycle might happen. This framework points to linkages that have the potential to elucidate how actors make

FIGURE 2.3 *Instructional capacity building framework*

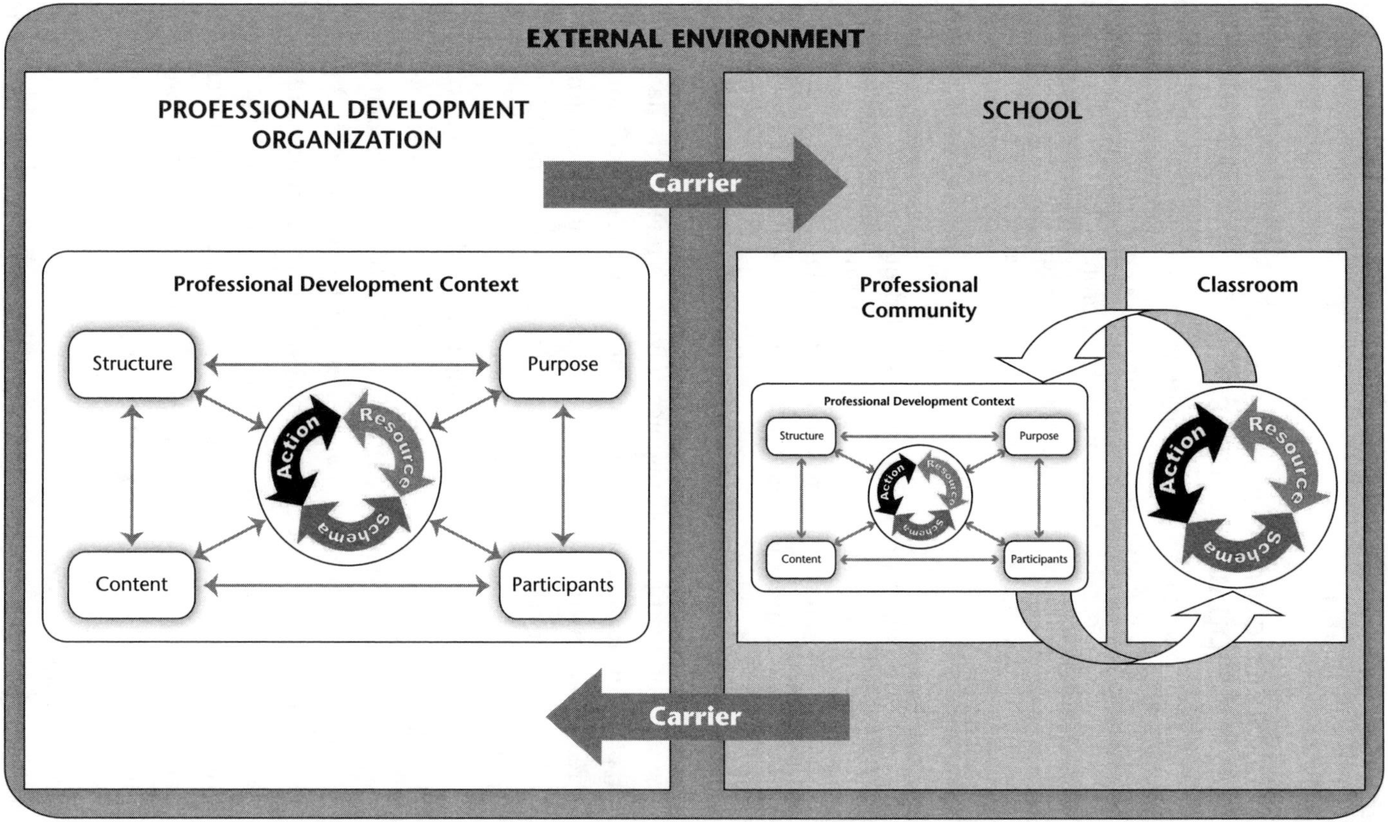

instructional decisions and judgments. It also depicts pathways along which instructional resources may travel; the implied carriers of these resources are educators, who are also the conveyors of ideas regarding resource use. For this aspect of the framework I draw upon the work of institutional and organizational scholars who study idea movement and the mechanisms of diffusion.

These pathways are the backdrop for the discussions in chapters 3 through 6. The two "carrier" arrows show bidirectional resource flows because instructional resources reside both within and outside of the school community and have the potential to flow into, through, and out of a school context. Therefore, a classroom teacher who is also a member of a grade-level team or subject-area department has at least two potential learning environments in which to gather and/or generate instructional resources and to test their use (e.g., the classroom and grade-level or department meetings). If this same teacher is also a participant in an external professional development program (or member of an external network) that convenes regularly during the year, this teacher may also carry any number of instructional resources between and among these contexts. This teacher then becomes a "carrier" of instructional resources. Whether or not the ideas or resources that she carries are adopted by others depends on a complex set of structural and sociocultural factors, including who the carrier is, her role and status within the community, how the resources are delivered, and the context into which they arrive.[4]

Context Boundaries and Intersections

Wenger theorized that the nature of the boundaries delineating communities of practice would influence the flow of ideas and the opportunities for learning by providing more (or fewer) opportunities for various contexts to influence one another. His work helps us think about how boundaries might differ among these communities and why the differences matter. Wenger distinguishes between two types of "edges" that communities of practice have: boundaries and peripheries.[5] He describes "boundaries" as lines that separate inside from outside and "peripheries" as areas of overlap and connection. How a school-based community defines itself, and whether it draws distinct boundaries around its work or seeks to develop connections to the rest of school—whether or not its edges resemble boundaries or peripheries—will affect the extent of resource use that occurs within that community and the sort of resource adoption that the community can stimulate beyond its borders. For example, at Cedar Bridge the sixth-grade humanities team worked in close proximity to the other subject-area teams; they all met in the library. They were engaged in similar activities (such as, answering the same questions to produce their meeting notes) and were often invited at the end of the session to share their team's insights with the other teams. These professional learning community practices opened up opportunities for learning and thus created peripheries, rather than solid boundaries, around the Cedar Bridge teams.

Wenger has also described how the borders of communities of practice can invite or repel participation: "Practice can be guarded just as it can be made available; membership can seem a daunting prospect just as it can constitute a welcoming invitation; a community of practice can be a fortress just as it can be an open door."[6]

Thus Wenger identifies a dimension of a community of practice—its openness to new ideas, people, and practices—that affects how likely instructional resources are to get identified, used, and generated. As Wenger explains, the boundaries of a community of practice have an important function in encouraging the arrival of new ideas and the adoption of instructional resources.

> On the one hand, communities of practice are learning assets through the depth of engagement they develop, but the locality of engagement entails the liability that useful connections beyond the boundaries of any given practice may not be apparent or sought. On the other hand, carefully managing boundaries by fostering boundary encounters helps prevent the deepening of communities from evolving into stale inbreeding or a source of excessive fragmentation. Instead, it allows that deepening to create new opportunities for learning.[7]

Wenger describes how the depth of engagement in a community can become a "learning asset" or, in my nomenclature, an instructional organizational resource for participants. The depth of the community of practice that existed among the sixth-grade humanities team at Cedar Bridge suggests that it was a learning asset for its participants and possibly for the school. Although depth of engagement in a community of practice is not easily achieved, Wenger also warns that if professional community is separated and isolated, resources for learning become severely limited. Therefore, he proposes "carefully managing boundaries by fostering boundary encounters."[8] The cross-team opportunities for sharing insights that Cedar Bridge orchestrated at the end of the professional learning community meetings are an example of what Wenger might call a boundary encounter.

Boundary Encounters

Wenger suggests two types of connections that exist between communities and can facilitate boundary encounters: boundary objects and brokering. Wenger defines boundary objects as "the artifacts, documents, terms, concepts and other forms of reification around which communities of practice can organize their interconnections."[9] For example, at Cedar Bridge we can imagine the grade-level teams organizing their interconnections around their use of talking-to-the-text. As previously described, the reifications that emerge are types of instructional resources (e.g., the text talk on the sticky notes). Wenger defines brokering as "connections provided by people who can introduce elements of practice into another."[10] Wenger's conceptual discussion of boundary objects and the act of brokering does not fully specify how each functions in practice. As the chapters in part 2 will show, the instructional capacity building framework illuminates the conditions that allow for boundary objects in the form of instructional resources to get taken up, used, and generated as well as the conditions that enable (or impede) resource carrying from one location to another.

Boundary Spanners

In the field of organizational studies, brokers are referred to as boundary spanners and carriers.[11] Institutional theorist Richard W. Scott has argued that there are various types of carriers and that "carriers are not neutral vehicles but have important effects on the elements transmitted."[12] He has suggested a typology of carriers that sorts them into four broad classes: symbolic systems, relational systems, routines, and artifacts.[13] He uses this classification to offer a way to think about what kinds of information various carrying mechanisms are likely to convey. For instance, which sorts of routines communicate regulative, normative, or cultural-cognitive information? Scott suggests that a routine such as "standard operating procedures" typically relay regulative information, whereas job descriptions or "roles" typically convey normative information, and "scripts" impart cultural-cognitive ideas.[14]

At Cedar Bridge, we can imagine different routines that might carry these different types of information. For instance, we can imagine that there were routines for conducting standardized tests (regulative); routines for how the subject-area, grade-level teams assembled in the library to examine student work samples from common formative assessments (normative); and routines or patterns of conversation (cultural-cognitive) that occurred within each individual teacher team. Each of these different types of routine conveys different sorts of information. Each type of routine presumably will incorporate particular instructional resources to varying degrees.

Scott's typology of "carriers" was developed from an institutional perspective and does not include people as a separate category of carriers. In my own research, however, I am particularly interested in the human carriers of instructional resources. How these resources get used is partly a function of the way in which the resources are conveyed—by whom, when, and how—as well as a function of the organizational context into which they arrive. Hence, in chapter 3 I consider the role of a teacher as an instructional resource carrier. In chapter 6, the role of principal as a resource carrier is examined as a particular sort of boundary spanner.

Various research literatures have looked at the role of boundary spanners in different ways. The knowledge management literature describes organizational boundaries, usually defined by the organization or work units within the organization; it also describes "boundary spanning" roles that individuals or groups can play, either officially or unofficially.[15] Traditionally, these boundary roles have been viewed as performing two types of functions: (1) processing information for the organization and

(2) representing the organization to the external world.[16] In Scott's terms, these boundary-spanning roles in the organizational literature are conceived of in primarily regulative and normative terms.

The knowledge management, institutional, and organizational literatures discuss the dual function that boundary spanners play, acting as both filters and facilitators of information.[17] These various research literatures, however, provide limited information on the microprocesses by which boundary spanners "broker" or "carry" information or resources.[18]

Boundary spanners need not only be individuals. They can also be teams or units. In many businesses, there are entire divisions that serve boundary-spanning functions, such as marketing groups or R&D units.[19] Research and design teams are viewed as playing an important boundary-spanning role.[20] Boundary spanning can even apply to whole organizations. For instance, the growing literature on intermediary organizations in the nonprofit field talks about the boundary spanning or bridging role that such organizations play as they mediate between two parties to facilitate change.[21] Thus, boundary spanners are individuals with connections to various contexts or who have membership in multiple communities. In school districts, some district office departments serve a boundary-spanning function. For instance, the team of district elementary school supervisors whose work is the subject of chapter 5 serve a boundary-spanning function to some degree. However, as chapter 6 indicates in its description of the district context in which the administrators work, the district does not capitalize on their boundary-spanning role.

Instructional Resource Carriers

Resource carriers are a particular type of boundary spanner who carry instructional resources from one location to another. What enables boundary spanners to become instructional resource carriers in educational environments? Tushman and Scanlan's study, in which they distinguish two types of boundary spanners, contributes a great deal to our understanding of who this special sort of boundary spanner is.[22] Beyond describing boundary spanners as connected internally and externally, they describe several other characteristics of an "informational boundary spanner." Informational boundary spanners are perceived by their colleagues to have technical competence; they may or may not have formal status within the organization or subunit.[23] These boundary spanners are also able "to translate across communication boundaries and be aware of contextual information on both sides of the boundary."[24] An instructional resource carrier in education, then, is what Tushman and Scanlan define as an informational boundary spanner in business organizations.

In addition to the criteria Tushman and Scanlan identify as necessary for carrying information, an instructional resource carrier may also have intimate knowledge of how a particular resource can be used. Although knowledge of resource use may facilitate the adoption of an instructional resource, a resource carrier with particular knowledge and/or instructional relationships will not ensure use of the "carried resource" by others. (This idea is explored in chapter 3.) Thus, examining the relationships between the carrier, the resource, and the context dimensions is helpful in order to understand when a carried resource is likely to get adopted. The following questions may be useful to ask:

- Is there a need in that context for that particular resource?
- Is this need understood, recognized, and shared by the community of potential users?
- Do other relevant knowledge, relational, and organizational resources exist in that setting to assist in the adoption and fitting of the carried resource to the new context?

The answers to these questions help reveal the sorts of conditions that are needed for resource use, resource creation, and resource carrying.

The specific examples in part 2 illuminate these processes in various settings. The instructional capacity building framework proposes processes that can stimulate learning through the use and generation of instructional resources, and brings attention to particular processes that have the potential to influence the identification, use, and creation of instructional resources. Such processes include the arrival of instructional resources into a context, the identification of instructional resources, and the process of fitting instructional resources into a particular setting.

SUMMARY

These first two chapters have laid out a set of conceptual ideas about what instructional capacity is, how it develops, and the role of resource carriers. Chapter 1 provided a conceptual framework to help direct attention to the location and processes in which instructional resources get identified for use and the conditions under which these resources are likely to be used. In this chapter, I presented a typology of resource use. I also explained the process of fitting the instructional resource to a particular context, which is essential for adapting, sustaining, and transforming or creating resources for purposeful instruction. Finally, I defined and described the role of resource carrier as a mechanism by which instructional resources are conveyed from one instructional setting to another.

Looking ahead, part 2 contains specific examples of how instructional resources get identified and used. Chapters 3 and 4 identify more precisely the conditions that are likely to stimulate the meaningful use of instructional resources by teachers. Chapters 5 and 6 offer examples of how a central office can help principals become effective resource carriers and foster conditions in their schools for continuous instructional improvement. Chapter 7 examines the sorts of conditions that are needed within the central office for continuous instructional resourcing to occur. All of these examples consider the ways boundaries are drawn around communities of practice in educational settings, as well as the intersection of external and school-based professional development communities, and the boundary spanners who act as instructional resource carriers between communities of practice.

PART II

INTEGRATING THEORY AND PRACTICE

CHAPTER 3

HOW DO TEACHERS USE INSTRUCTIONAL RESOURCES?

Maisey, Molly, Will, and Pat

This chapter attempts to deepen our understanding of the conditions that influence teachers' use of instructional technology. I explore the conditions that seem to make it more likely that teachers will actually use particular methods and materials in their teaching—and in a way that improves students' opportunities to learn—by providing portraits of teaching. We will look closely at four teachers who taught sixth-grade English and history in two neighboring middle schools with comparable student demographics.[1] Teachers Maisey and Molly taught English and history at Cedar Bridge Middle School; teachers Will and Pat taught history at Liberty Middle School. All four teachers also participated in the same professional development program (Reading Apprenticeship) in which they were taught specific strategies for teaching reading comprehension to adolescent students. How these teachers used the particular instructional strategies for teaching reading can help us determine the conditions that influence teachers' use of instructional technology resources. (Chapter 4 provides a comparative analysis that examines the learning conditions in each of the two schools.)

CONDITIONS THAT INFLUENCE TEACHERS' USE OF A SPECIFIC INSTRUCTIONAL METHOD

Four teachers—Maisey, Molly, Will, and Pat—were introduced to the same instructional technology, a research-based approach to teaching reading comprehension strategies to adolescents.[2] They attended a three-day Reading Apprenticeship (RA) professional development workshop in the summer and then participated in four days of additional professional development spread out across the year that focused on how to use this instructional method in their teaching. The RA program followed the principles of effective professional development (PD) design. It included seven full days of training with online support available between the RA sessions. RA encouraged its participants to attend the program with school colleagues and to use the RA instructional methods in their teaching. All participating schools were asked to identify a site-based Reading Apprenticeship leader who was tasked with organizing school participants to attend follow-up sessions and complete their RA assignments. For example, participating teachers were asked to bring samples of student reading comprehension work along with their teaching experiences to PD sessions for discussion and analysis. Although all four teachers attended the same RA training and taught similar course content to sixth-grade students, their use of RA instructional technology differed considerably. The differences in their use of the instructional technology are instructive and are the focus of this chapter.

The Instructional Technology: Talking-to-the-Text

To understand the conditions under which a resource is likely to get used, it is helpful to know something about the original purpose and design of the instructional technology. Talking-to-the-text is a signature method of the reading instruction program created by the Strategic Literacy Initiative at WestEd.[3] According to RA program directors, RA "combines affective and cognitive aspects of literacy support [to promote] adolescents' engagement and achievement in reading and writing in their content-area classes." Designed for middle school and high school teachers across subject-area domains, the program developed materials and tools, such as talking-to-the-text, to support teacher and student learning.

RA takes the stance that a reader's judgment—his particular skills, knowledge, and purposes for reading—ought to determine how he talks to the text. Thus, the RA tools and methods are intentionally not scripted. RA teaches that setting a purpose for reading is an important cognitive skill for readers to develop. A related RA idea is that "proficient readers read texts differently depending on their purposes for reading." For instance, a reader might read the opening paragraph of a text and then stop to think about how the narrative voice, topic, and point of view are evident. Talking-to-the-text frames the conception that thinking and reading are intertwined, and this instructional routine asks readers to become aware of their thinking in preparation for, during, and after reading a text.

Given RA's stance toward reading, there were no worksheets or scripted set of procedures for a reader to follow. The talking-to-the-text approach highlighted the idea that the reader should document his thinking about the text since this cognitive process affects the reader's overall understanding of the text; the approach also asserts that text talk provides important information about a reader's thinking that can and should inform reading instruction. For these reasons, this particular instructional technology resource provides an instructional method (software) but has few accompanying tools (hardware).

This design has both advantages and drawbacks for a teacher who is just learning to use the routine. How effectively talking-to-the-text is used by a teacher depends on the user's grasp of the method as well as a clear understanding of the specific purpose for reading a particular text at a given time. For example, for a teacher to use this method with students, the teacher has to explain what she wants students to do; there is no worksheet to hand out with instructions for students to follow. On the surface, this instructional resource may seem easy to use. Yet novice users in RA professional development sessions sometimes asked for prescribed steps or a scripted routine. A frequent question was: What sorts of things should students write down?

Any teacher who wants to use talking-to-the-text effectively as an instructional strategy needs sufficient knowledge—of the particular text that a student is responding to and of the reader's reading skills—and a clear instructional purpose for using the strategy. If a teacher has sufficient knowledge of the instructional technology, of her students, and an instructional purpose, then the teacher can make meaningful decisions about how to help readers use talking-to-the-text as a meaning-making strategy.

Limited Knowledge Leads to Perfunctory Use of Resources

The four teachers described in this chapter appeared to have different levels of understanding regarding how to use this instructional approach in their teaching. Maisey and Molly were both new teachers at Cedar Bridge, and Molly was also a first-year teacher. They had attended the three-day RA professional development program in August prior to the start of school. Each recognized that RA was "a big focus" at Cedar Bridge and so began to use the RA strategies in their classrooms at the beginning of the school year. They had their students use the talking-to-the-text routine. However, their initial use of the routine indicated that neither Maisey nor Molly had a deep understanding of the RA technology, its underlying principles, or of how this instructional approach connected to their instructional goals.

TEACHER PORTRAITS

Maisey's Experience

Maisey did not have a deep understanding of the RA technology or of talking-to-the-text in particular. She said, "It's kind of my gut instinct to want to do a lot of read-aloud with [my students] and me reading to them." Maisey explained her inclination to read to her students as stemming from her observation that students "seem to like it better when I read aloud to them, but they also seem engaged." Maisey lacked a sophisticated rationale for this instructional decision. By choosing to read to her students instead of having them read, she did not give her students practice with how to negotiate meaning while reading. Maisey recognized this problem but still found it "hard . . . letting go."

[The instructional coach, Lydia] always uses the [analogy] . . . *if you give a man a fish, he eats for a day; if you teach a man how to fish, he eats forever.* . . . Lydia always uses that example for me because . . . I told her that, you know, I feel like probably the students' comprehension is higher when I read to them and stop and check in or when they read aloud than when we do a whole-class read-aloud.

Maisey knew that there were RA strategies, like partner reading and talking-to-the-text, that were designed to help students increase their comprehension while reading, but she felt like she needed to learn more about these strategies before she could use them. As she put it, "I feel like I need to become more—just educated on some—I just need to do a little, I think—I just need to learn some of the—just so I have them internalized, or, like, just do a little learning myself about, like, good strategies and talk to some other teachers."

The hesitation and faltering we hear in her explanation suggests the uncertainty she felt about how to start using the RA strategies. Did she know enough? Would the strategies work? Ultimately, Maisey said she would like to "incorporate [partner reading] a lot more." She was aware that her sixth-grade teaching colleague, Miranda, a veteran teacher in her sixth year at Cedar Bridge, "does that a lot" and said that Miranda "has a lot of routines" for teaching partner reading. Although Maisey knew that Miranda possessed a great deal of knowledge about how to use RA strategies, she did not seek out Miranda for help. Her reluctance to ask for help is not unusual. For a variety of reasons, teachers often do not consult their colleagues on staff even if they have relevant expertise in some aspect of instruction.[4] Teachers who do seek out colleagues for their instructional expertise, in the language of instructional capacity building, are developing instructional relationships.

Maisey's Resource Use Becomes More Intentional   As the year wore on, in part compelled to action by the culture of the Humanities Department, Maisey started to have students practice talking-to-the-text in her class "usually about once a week" when students read "a current event." Maisey said, "That's really . . . where I pick up the most on how students are talking to the text . . . I actually take [their work] home and look at it and see how they're talking to the text." Maisey described her growing capacity to put more RA technology into use in her instruction. However, she did not yet tightly connect her use of talking-to-the-text to her instructional goals. For instance, she did not give students feedback on their text talk on current events. When she did provide feedback on text talk, she did not give it systematically to all students.

> **Ann:** Do you give them feedback on their actual talk?
>
> **Maisey:** Not on their current event. I do on their history [reading] because I try to like help them see how what they're writing could help them understand, so I try to point that out. . . . It's one of those things where I'll go around to maybe one person at a table and I'll ask them why they wrote that or circled that or . . . it's much more on an informal level. I've never handed back something, maybe I should, but I've never handed back, like somebody talking to the text, and like had *them* reflect on what I wrote.

Although Maisey had her students practice talking-to-the-text regularly, she was "informal" in how she gave students feedback on the way they talked to the text or how their text talk connected to the big ideas in the course. She was aware that her approach to feedback was not systematic; thus her use of the strategy remained somewhat separated from her instructional goals and did not appear intentionally connected to individual student learning needs. There was also no evidence that students' use of talking-to-the-text informed Maisey's instructional decisions. Therefore, we might depict Maisey's use of talking-to-the-text on the resource use spectrum as shown in figure 3.1.

Maisey Lacks a Deep Understanding of the Purpose That Underlies Talking-to-the-Text   Maisey's use of talking-to-the-text remained at the level of putting an activity into use without a deep understanding of the purpose and principles that underlay the method. This is a common problem of implementation. Researchers Milbrey McLaughlin and Dana Mitra suggest that the source of this problem stems from a lack of understanding of the change theory underlying the particular reform, in this case talking-to-the-text.[5] McLaughlin and Mitra suggest, "Teachers need to

FIGURE 3.1   *Maisey's use of talking-to-the-text on the resource use spectrum*

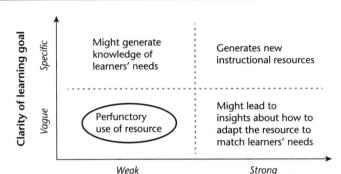

know, understand and enact the first principles that constitute the grammar of the reform—not only the activities or practices associated with it."[6] A first principle of the RA strategies is that reading and thinking are intertwined and that making thinking visible while reading has implications for learning and teaching. As the portraits of resource use in this chapter will show, "Implementation is both assimilation and construction, and must be anchored in general reform principles and concrete teaching contexts."[7]

Molly's Experience

A first-year teacher, Molly also began using talking-to-the-text and other RA methods at the beginning of the year. Like Maisey, she used these resources without connecting them to her instructional goals and with little understanding of the "first principles" underlying the RA approach to teaching reading. At the beginning of the year, Molly said, "I didn't really have to teach them [RA strategies]" since they were widely used at Cedar Bridge. In October, Molly said:

I was actually really surprised by how good [my students] were at [talking-to-the-text] in the beginning, and I think it really helps that . . . I didn't really have to teach them very much about [talking-to-the-text] because of the Academic Literacy Class that most of them take, and so a lot of them were very used to it already or they'd gotten schooling on it.

Seeing no need to provide students with instruction on this method, Molly assigned talking-to-the-text for homework. At first, she did not seem to understand that the instructional value of talking-to-the-text was *in its particular use*: how students engaged in the process of talking-to-the-text was related to the quality of text talk that they produced, and teaching students how to use this strategy was a way to teach students how to think about their reading.

Molly did notice differences in her students' ability to talk to the text. "Some students do a really great job with it," she noted. Those students seemed to understand that talking-to-the-text provided an opportunity to interact with and respond to a text, whereas others appeared to have a superficial or mechanical understanding of the process. In spite of perceiving these differences in her students' use of the strategy, Molly thought all her students had "learned" how to use this tool already and therefore did not need further instruction.

With this assumption, Molly also revealed her own novice understanding about teaching reading and of how to use the RA instructional technology to support her teaching: "I don't know how to . . . bridge [my reading aloud] to them learning to [read independently] . . . or becoming a better reader . . . it's just so hard, with so many students in your class, to focus on individual students." In the fall semester, as her comment revealed, Molly did not know how to use talking-to-the-text (or other RA strategies) to help her provide individualized support to students or to help them become better readers. Like Maisey, Molly used talking-to-the-text in a perfunctory manner.

Both Maisey and Molly had students do the activity of talking-to-the-text, but they did not connect their use of this method to specific instructional goals. They were not fitting the method to students' particular needs, or using the strategy intentionally to deepen students' understanding of the course content. Their use of talking-to-the-text was limited. Their efforts reveal that learning how to use this particular instructional technology (and, I posit, any instructional resource) to improve teaching and student learning requires using the resource with specific learning goals in mind. It also requires assessing how well the use of the resource in that context is achieving the instructional goal(s).

Will's Experience

In nearby Liberty Middle School, Will, a sixth-grade history teacher, was also experimenting with the use of talking-to-the-text in his classroom. Over the summer Will had attended the same RA professional development as Maisey and Molly. His initial approach to using talking-to-the-text, however, was quite intentional: "I'm just making an effort every week to be touching on it [RA strategies] and doing something explicit." His motivation to persist in the use of RA strategies came from his strong belief that reading was a "gatekeeper" skill and a portal for thinking. Will told his students that talking-to-the-text "is not about knowing; it is just about thinking." Will saw RA strategies as a way to help students recognize that texts have layers of meaning: "If you're not even aware of that structure, then you can't really access it . . . It's like by chance that you have a deep question." Will wanted his students to see nuances, to distinguish between "shallow" and "deep" understanding and to recognize the complexity within subject matter. By midyear, he had seen improvement in students' test scores. "Doing [talking-to-the-text] over and over again . . . helped them . . . figure out . . . what matters in the [test] question[s]." He also credited his use of RA strategies with helping students to have "philosophical conversations" and to distinguish between "what are universal questions and what are specific questions."

Specific instructional purposes undergirded Will's use of RA instructional resources, and he wanted his students to similarly appropriate a purpose for using these thinking tools. For instance, Will told his students that "some people find talking-to-the-text hard and others love it, but we do it for a reason. Why?" He emphasized the goal for using this reading strategy by creating lessons to develop students' purposeful appropriation of these RA tools. In one lesson, he asked students to reflect in writing on this question: Why do we practice talking to the text? When students finished their written reflections, they were asked to talk with each other to find out how "we are viewing talking-to-the-text" in this class. As students exchanged their views, a shared purpose for using talking-to-the-text emerged. One student articulated the purpose this way: "We practice talking-to-the-text so that we can understand the text better." Through this activity and others, Will's class developed a shared and public commitment to using strategies for making meaning while reading. The culture of thinking in Will's classroom was palpable and the purpose for reading was explicit.

Will's instructional moves—fitting the use of RA strategies to his students' needs and developing a shared purpose with his students for using these tools—seemed instinctive. He also recognized other ways in which he needed to connect his use of RA resources to his course content.

> Something that I noticed with my teaching is that last year I focused a lot on content. . . . I actually believe that sixth grade is more about skill but, once again, I had this disjointed, thought-matching process . . . because I assessed content, but I didn't assess skill. . . . Then I looked at the RA stuff and [something clicked] . . . skills are important, but I'm not assessing them so I need to do that.

Will recognized the need to fit his use of these strategies to the particular needs of the individual students in his classroom, help students use these routines effectively, and hold them responsible for using them. He was never explicitly taught to fit these strategies to his classroom through the RA program, nor did he receive support from his colleagues or administrators at Liberty to do so.

Three of Will's sixth-grade colleagues participated in the RA professional development with him. Only one was also a history department colleague—his grade-level partner, Pat. She, however, did not really use RA strategies in her teaching. The administrator at Liberty who supported the history department had only "heard about" RA. She had a "general idea of what it is but not real specifically." So, Will's persistent use of talking-to-the-text was self-driven. He engaged in an iterative process of fitting the RA methods and tools to his instructional goals and students' needs because he believed the RA instructional technology could help him better teach the knowledge and skills he wanted his students to learn. Will's approach to using the RA resources differed from Maisey's and Molly's. Recall that initially Molly didn't think she needed to teach the talking-to-the-text process because her students had learned the method in another class.

Pat's Experience

Although Pat, Will's colleague, also attended the RA professional development, she did not really use the RA strategies with her students. Pat said she was attracted to the RA professional development program because she wanted to place more emphasis on reading instruction in her history class, but she claimed that "there is a disconnect between my belief system and my practice." Pat espoused the need for content teachers to provide literacy instruction to middle school students. However, she said, "I don't find myself doing that very much yet, and . . . I took RA because of that." In June, Pat reflected upon why she had not used the RA instructional resources that much.

> I feel that I want to go much deeper and I haven't. I don't think that I've taken the RA training as deep as I need to in order to have really benefited from it. I think the reason for that has to do with having a competing set of expectations and that the things that I was assessing the students on are not necessarily directly aligned with RA. So even though I feel philosophically committed to it, I just . . . yeah, I just had another set of priorities that ended up limiting how much time I spent in terms of trying to implement it . . . that and, well, there's other reasons. When I reflect on the whole piece, what I would do differently would have been to have the group of people [from Liberty] who trained together, meet together in between the trainings and really talk about . . . what we've tried, the difficulties we've had . . . set some goals together or at least set individual goals and use the group as a way to keep ourselves moving on it and to offer each other some feedback or support.

Pat viewed the gap between her espoused beliefs and enacted practice as a partial failure of the existing school supports. For her, the RA follow-up sessions were an insufficient incentive to support her in changing her daily instructional practice.

In addition, Pat offered two other possible impediments to her use of the RA technology. One was the course textbook. She thought it "doesn't challenge the students very much and so I can't really . . . use the textbook as a text that is going to help them learn to analyze difficult text because it's not that difficult." Could Pat have found alternative or supplementary texts for her students to read? Could someone else have helped with this need? Second, Pat said that her teaching partner, Will, "has a different teaching style than me, and he is much more about presenting visual things . . . and so when we plan, we tend not to use . . . any text very much."

Pat seemed to indicate that she needed a different kind of support and guidance than the seven days of professional development could provide. The array of constraints that she identified—different conceptions of instruction and instructional purposes, the absence of appropriate texts, and a lack of organizational structures in the school to support talking with her RA colleagues—all point to Pat's need for assistance in *fitting* the instructional technology to her own teaching context. Pat needed different and more supportive school-based conditions that could provide her with greater guidance in using RA technology purposefully with her students. After all, she claimed that she wanted to use these resources. She recognized there was a "disconnect" between her beliefs and actions.

PURPOSEFUL USE OF INSTRUCTIONAL TECHNOLOGY CAN GENERATE INSTRUCTIONAL KNOWLEDGE

Ultimately, the manner in which both Will and Molly used talking-to-the-text and other RA resources generated instructional knowledge: information about their students as readers and learners as well as pedagogical content knowledge about teaching reading and assessing reading comprehension. Over time, with continued use and opportunities for feedback, Molly learned to use the reading strategies more purposefully. For example, as she got clearer about her instructional purpose for using talking-to-the-text, she gained specific information about her students' learning needs. In a reciprocal manner, as she learned more about her students' reading and thinking-while-reading behaviors, she developed ways to adapt her use of talking-to-the-text so that the method better fit what her students needed to learn. Her process of fitting this instructional method to her instructional goal and to the specific needs of the students led her to use other RA methods and tools. (Chapter 4 describes how Cedar Bridge supported Molly in making these instructional adjustments.)

When instructional technology is not used in a purposeful way and is not tied to specific student learning goals, instructional knowledge is unlikely to be generated. For instance, Maisey persisted in her use of talking-to-the-text. She tinkered with her approach and made some minor adjustments to how she used the routine with her students, but she never explicitly connected her use of this technology to specific learning goals. There was no evidence that her use of the routine generated new knowledge about her students or improved her instruction.

DEEP UNDERSTANDING OF INSTRUCTIONAL TECHNOLOGY ENABLES ITS PURPOSEFUL USE

The discussion of how Will used talking-to-the-text, in comparison to Maisey and Molly, reveals the significance of having a deep understanding of the instructional resource and its underlying theory of learning. This understanding helped Will figure out how to use talking-to-the-text effectively. He taught the underlying purpose of talking-to-the-text to his students and thus empowered them with this knowledge. Unlike his colleague Pat, Will described making an effort to do something "explicit" with the reading strategies each week because he saw their preeminent importance. He changed the assessments in his course so that students' reading skills were assessed, whereas Pat explained that she did not use the RA strategies because "the things that [she] was assessing the students on [were] not necessarily directly aligned to the [reading strategies]."

Will was able to figure out how to fit the instructional technology to his instructional goals. Indeed, his depth of understanding of the RA philosophy seemed to help him reorient the focus of his sixth-grade history course to develop these reading and thinking skills in his students; the historical content was no longer the singular or primary content because he recognized that effective thinking and reading skills were critical "gatekeeper" skills. Will demonstrated his capacity to teach analytic thinking and reading skills as well as a recognition that his students needed to learn these skills. Will possessed this instructional knowledge of content, of pedagogy, and of his students. His colleague Pat did not.

Neither Maisey nor Molly started the year with Will's depth of instructional knowledge, but with ongoing support at their school, Molly was able to develop her instructional knowledge. Maisey persisted in her use of talking-to-the-text and although she did not make progress as quickly as Molly did, it is possibile that with the continued use of the resource and ongoing, intentional support, her instructional knowledge also might deepen over time. Most teachers are not like Will. They need some sort of ongoing support to be able to use new instructional methods, or other instructional resources, in a way that actually advances student learning. Or, as was the case with Pat, teachers need support in how to fit the use of the resource into their teaching in a meaningful way so that they can persist in its use and thus develop their instructional skills.

SEEING THE PD KNOWLEDGE TRANSFER PROBLEM ANEW

One reason that so little transfers from professional development experiences into teachers' classrooms, even from PD programs like RA that involve seven days of professional development training across a school year, is because few schools provide the necessary learning supports to teachers who are trying to use new instructional routines and tools in their classrooms. In hindsight, for example, Pat thought that different school supports would have made a difference in her ability to use talking-to-the-text in her teaching. Molly credited the supports that Cedar Bridge provided with enabling her to develop her capacity to use talking-to-the-text, which she said increased her instructional knowledge, including her understanding of her students' strengths, interests, and needs.

There are many reasons schools often don't provide sufficient supports for teachers to use PD content (i.e., instructional knowledge and technology) when they return to their classrooms. These include

1. *Lack of knowledge about the PD resource*: School leaders may not know enough about the particular instructional approach or PD content to understand its potential value to improve teaching and learning or to determine if additional investment in this professional knowledge is worthwhile.
2. *Lack of knowledge about what adult learning requires*: School leaders may not understand the necessity of providing teachers with support and structured opportunities to intentionally practice the use of a new skill and receive feedback.
3. *Lack of know-how*: School leaders may not know how to structure meaningful organizational learning supports.
4. *Lack of resources*: School leaders may not have (or think they don't have) the necessary resources (time, money, personnel, or expertise) to provide such supports to teachers.

These problems of school learning environments are considered, along with some solutions, in chapter 4: "How Does Instructional Capacity Grow Within Schools?"

CHAPTER 4

HOW DOES INSTRUCTIONAL CAPACITY GROW WITHIN SCHOOLS?

Cedar Bridge and Liberty Middle Schools

This chapter looks beyond teachers' classroom use of instructional technology to the schools' role in helping teachers to identify appropriate instructional technology and use it effectively. In other words, how can schools (including groups of teachers, such as grade-level teams or departments) expand their capacity for adult learning so that both teaching and student learning can improve? The improvement of teaching and learning is defined as the intentional and observable changes to teachers' instruction with the overall aim of strengthening learning outcomes for students.[1] In chapter 3, for example, teachers Will (Liberty) and Molly (Cedar Bridge) were each described as using Reading Apprenticeship (RA) instructional strategies in intentional ways aimed at strengthening student learning.

To advance our understanding of *how* schools can grow their institutional instructional capacity, in this chapter we consider the Cedar Bridge and Liberty Middle School approaches to identifying and supporting professional development and the use of instructional resources. These two middle schools served similar populations of students. Cohorts of teachers from both schools attended the same RA professional development program. Yet a close look at the sort of learning opportunities provided to teachers within the two schools reveals important differences. These differences illuminate specific conditions needed to support teachers' ongoing and collective learning. The school descriptions highlight the actions taken by school leaders and teachers that affected the school's capacity for instructional improvement.

TWO SCHOOLS ON DIFFERENT TRAJECTORIES FOR BUILDING INSTRUCTIONAL CAPACITY

Cedar Bridge and Liberty were neighboring middle schools.[2] They were both located in the Timberland Unified School District in a city of approximately four hundred thousand people. Both schools served large populations of low-income, minority students. Although there were more African American students at Cedar Bridge (42% versus 31%) and more white students at Liberty (11% versus 2%), the student demographics were comparable (see the breakdown in table 4.1).

Both schools had a caring principal at the helm committed to educating his or her students. Both principals were committed to teacher collaboration and went to significant effort to create opportunities for teachers

TABLE 4.1 *Demographic characteristics of case study schools*

SCHOOL	NUMBER OF STUDENTS	RACE/ETHNICITY	FREE/ REDUCED LUNCH	ENGLISH LANGUAGE LEARNERS	SPECIAL EDUCATION
Liberty	691	African American (31%) Asian (37%) Latino (16%) Filipino (2%) Pacific Islander (1%) White (11%) Other (3%)	59.6%	11%	15.6%
Cedar Bridge	610	African American (42%) Asian (34%) Latino (18%) Filipino (1%) White (2%) American Indian (1%) Other (1%)	74.8%	20%	19.3%

to meet together. In so doing, each principal sought to grow the school's capacity for instructional improvement. Both principals also attended the same professional development conference focused on developing professional learning communities in schools. Additionally, the sixth- and eighth-grade English and history teachers, who were interviewed and observed as part of a year-long professional development study in these two schools, participated in the same two professional development programs: Reading Apprenticeship (RA) and Cultural Linguistic Instruction (CLI), a program that focused on culturally and linguistically responsive instruction.[3] These commonalities make comparing these schools particularly interesting.

The two school portraits that follow show how each school went about trying to create conditions for instructional improvement but achieved different results. The portraits reveal the dynamic interplay between the actions the two principals took and their different beliefs about teaching and learning (i.e., their schema), and how these actions ultimately affected their identification, selection, and use of instructional resources. Significant differences in the growth of instructional capacity at the two schools emerged, as indicated by changes to teachers' instruction and to the substance of their professional conversations with each other. The sections below offer a detailed description of each school's attempts to increase instructional capacity. The instructional capacity building framework illuminates the particular actions, ideas, and use of instructional resources that expanded instructional capacity at Cedar Bridge and detracted from its growth at Liberty.

THE LEARNING EVNIRONMENT AT CEDAR BRIDGE MIDDLE SCHOOL

Cedar Bridge Middle School served approximately six hundred sixth-through eighth-grade students. Its student body was ethnically diverse. Most students (75%) were eligible for free and/or reduced-price lunch. In the mornings before school began, the cafeteria was filled with students eating cereal and drinking half-pint cartons of milk. Teachers at Cedar Bridge, the majority of whom were white, were committed to the school's "ultimate goal . . . of reducing the achievement gap [that existed] between the African American and Latino kids and all other [students]" at the school. Cedar Bridge staff believed it was their responsibility to create an environment in which each student could learn. The administration saw a close connection between establishing a meaningful learning environment for teachers and creating a supportive learning environment for students. These institutional values and beliefs shaped the manner in which Cedar Bridge identified opportunities for teacher professional learning and brought these opportunities to teachers. The leaders' beliefs and values influenced the ways the school supported teachers to continuously improve *how* they taught students.

When I first arrived at Cedar Bridge Middle School, I found the school had already accumulated significant instructional resources through sustained efforts, capable leadership, and the longevity of the staff. I describe examples of each type of instructional resource that were available at the outset of my study. As the analysis that follows will show, Cedar Bridge used all of its instructional resources to continue building its instructional capacity as it sought ways to improve the learning outcomes for its lowest performing Latino and African American students.[4]

An Overview of Available Instructional Resources at Cedar Bridge

Instructional Knowledge   *Instructional knowledge resources* refer to knowledge of content, pedagogy, and students. Over a seven-year period, Cedar Bridge steadily invested time and money in developing teachers' knowledge of teaching reading to adolescents. Specifically, the school did this by sending teams of teachers to participate in the nationally recognized professional development program Reading Apprenticeship, which targets adolescent literacy. According to the Cedar Bridge principal, Seymore Everett, "Every new teacher, we want to try and get on board [with RA] right away. . . . Ideally, we would have every new person be a part of the beginning networks . . . regardless of discipline." Cedar Bridge had sent teams of teachers from all subject areas to Reading Apprenticeship and had enrolled cohorts of teachers in RA's continuing Reading Apprenticeship network. As teachers new to Cedar Bridge, Maisey and Molly participated in the RA professional development.

In addition to sending teachers to the RA professional development, in previous years Cedar Bridge had developed complementary within-school professional development supports to help teachers use these literacy practices more effectively in their classrooms. Consequently, among veteran teachers at Cedar Bridge, there was a great deal of collective expertise in teaching reading to adolescents through their exposure to and use of RA tools and methods.

Cedar Bridge teachers also had developed a common curriculum for each grade level and had agreed upon a set of "essential standards" for student learning. According to the instructional coach, Lydia, a few years earlier Cedar Bridge "had department meetings twice a month," with the additional monthly department meeting used to "unpack the standards and write them in kid-friendly language." Through this process, Lydia said the Humanities Department distilled the essential elements of the language arts standards for use in their instructional planning and teaching. By the time I began my study at Cedar Bridge, the department had developed a shared set of beliefs about instruction and some common approaches to teaching. For example, teachers had agreed to use core texts and common assignments in their classes. As at many schools, these teachers also took efforts to get to know their students—their particular interests, strengths, and needs. The depth of instructional knowledge varied between subject departments and individual staff members. Ultimately, the supply of instructional knowledge within a department was largely influenced by the department leadership and teacher turnover. In the Humanities Department, only two of the seven sixth- and eighth-grade humanities teachers were new to Cedar Bridge.

Instructional Technology *Instructional technology* refers to the tools, materials, and methods of instruction that are used in a particular classroom, school, or district. As described, Cedar Bridge had a sustained emphasis on developing teachers' expertise in teaching reading to adolescents. The school's ongoing connections to the Reading Apprenticeship program and its site-based support to all teachers in how to use RA tools and methods in their classrooms meant that the RA philosophy was among the instructional technology resources available at Cedar Bridge. RA materials included various tools, routines, and frameworks for thinking about teaching reading as a meaning-making process. RA tools and methods included knowing students' reading habits, unveiling and demystifying the multiple dimensions of reading, using talking-to-the-text, having metacognitive conversations, and using the Question-Answer Relationship (QAR), Text Analysis Tool, and reciprocal teaching strategies. The purpose for these methods ("software") and their corresponding tools ("hardware"), to the extent that they existed, are described in table 4.2.

In addition to the instructional technology associated with Reading Apprenticeship, each subject-area department also had its own instructional technology in the form of curriculum, texts, subject-specific instructional approaches, assignments, and assessments that teachers used in their courses. At Cedar Bridge, instructional technology could be described as belonging to the department, rather than the individual teacher.

TABLE 4.2 *Reading Apprenticeship instructional technology*

INSTRUCTIONAL PURPOSE	"SOFTWARE"	ACCOMPANYING "HARDWARE"
Learn about students' histories as readers and their reading habits	Develop reader identities	Reader survey
Make students' thinking while reading visible	Use talking-to-the-text and think-aloud routines; facilitate metacognitive conversations: what did you do while reading to make sense of text?	Bookmark tool with questions to ask while reading; RA Reading Dimensions; framework: personal, social, cognitive, knowledge-building; RA binder of resources for teaching and relevant research articles
Provide strategies to increase comprehension and develop independence as readers	Use Question-Answer Relationship (QAR) routine and reciprocal teaching (RT)	QAR steps; reciprocal teaching steps; research articles describing QAR and RT in use
Provide strategies to develop disciplinary ways of reading and to activate prior knowledge	Conduct a text analysis; surface students' prior knowledge through the use of routines	Text analysis framework; vocabulary-building tool; research articles on these tools in use; LINK (List, Inquire, Note, and Know) procedures

Organizational Resources for Instruction   Cedar Bridge had many organizational structures that were intended to support instruction: department meetings and meetings for grade-level teachers who taught the same subject (e.g., sixth-grade humanities teachers); formal instructional roles designed to support instruction, such as instructional coaches and department chairs; professional development funds allocated to promote teachers' participation in professional development programs, such as RA; and a tradition of using staff meeting time to encourage instructional improvement, such as the series of staff meetings to help teachers use RA methods and tools in their classrooms. The organizational routines and practices with regard to instruction (e.g., Cedar Bridge's process for selecting professional development programs, or its focus on curricular planning during grade-level meetings) are examples of organizational resources that supported high-quality teaching at Cedar Bridge.

Relational Resources to Support Instruction   *Relational resources* that support instruction refer to the adult relationships in a school and the extent to which these relationships revolve around matters of teaching and learning. Learning is a social process. Therefore, educators need to be able to learn from one another if the school intends to increase its instructional capacity. The relationship between Lydia and Molly, for example, was an instructional relationship. If schools are to be learning environments for adults, those adults must have support to develop interpersonal relationships characterized by honest and direct conversations about their teaching tied to evidence of student learning. Educators also need to be able to discuss their teaching challenges with one another, as the sixth-grade humanities team did at Cedar Bridge. Teaching so that students learn is a deeply complex and dynamic process. Therefore, teachers need to engage in collective problem solving about various matters of teaching and learning. To have such conversations in a genuine manner requires trust and respect among educators as well as a reciprocal obligation to help one another.

The studies of the social organization of the teachers' workplace conducted by Susan Rosenholtz show that the manner in which teachers' work is organized can either encourage or dissuade teachers from collaborating.[5]

Furthermore, developing shared instructional goals, refining the use of a particular instructional technology for a specific learning purpose, and collaboratively examining student work for evidence of learning are ways to develop strong instructional relationships among educators.

At Cedar Bridge, the quality of educators' relationships (e.g., sense of trust, respect, and felt obligation to assist colleagues) as well as educators' perceptions of their colleagues' instructional expertise was evident in their interactions with each other. In the Humanities Department, there were several teachers who were perceived by their colleagues as strong, capable, and experienced. In addition, Lydia, who was an instructional coach and a former teacher at Cedar Bridge, was widely viewed by the staff as an excellent teacher with significant instructional expertise in teaching reading and writing to middle school students. Veteran and new teachers frequently sought her out for assistance, which she willingly provided. (Table 4.3 provides the names and roles of Cedar Bridge case study participants.) Significant relational resources existed within the Humanities Department as well as between the humanities teachers and the

TABLE 4.3   *Cedar Bridge case study participants*

NAME	ROLE	YEARS AT CEDAR BRIDGE
Seymore Everett	Principal	5
RJ Bookman	Assistant principal	3
Lydia Arachne[a,b]	Instructional coach	8
Miranda[b]	6th-grade humanities teacher	6
Maisey[a]	6th-grade humanities teacher	1
Molly[a]	6th-grade humanities teacher	1
Jessie[b]	8th-grade humanities teacher and visual arts teacher	7
Julie[b]	8th-grade humanities teacher	3
Jordan[b]	8th-grade humanities teacher	2
Francis Bowling[a,b]	Humanities dept. chair and academic literature teacher	9

Note: Cedar Bridge pseudonyms are multisyllabic names.
[a] Denotes RA participants at the time of the study.
[b] Denotes previous RA participants.

administrative staff. Cedar Bridge was well endowed with each type of instructional resource.

The Intentional Selection of Instructional Resources

The process by which Cedar Bridge identified and selected instructional resources for the staff influenced how they got used. At Cedar Bridge, administrators and sometimes teachers engaged in a dual process of identifying an instructional resource and simultaneously learning about that resource. For example, Cedar Bridge selected two professional development programs that would become the professional learning focus for the staff that year: (1) exploring ways to provide relevant Cultural Linguistic Instruction (CLI) to students and (2) designing and implementing a professional learning community (PLC) structure in the school. The manner in which these two programs were identified at Cedar Bridge, particularly who was involved and how learning about each resource became part of the selection process, suggests that Cedar Bridge leaders viewed selecting professional development as collective work and valued teachers' perspectives. The processes Cedar Bridge used to identify and select these two instructional resources also seemed to aid teachers in their use of the resources.

Identifying Cultural Linguistic Instruction at Cedar Bridge Lydia brought Cultural Linguistic Instruction to Seymore's attention two years before the school decided to introduce the resource to its staff. Lydia learned about CLI at a district-sponsored workshop and thought it could help Cedar Bridge tackle an identified problem: African American and Latino students demonstrated chronically low academic achievement. According to Seymore, "A year and a half ago . . . we noticed we hadn't been moving our African American kids at all. . . . The achievement gap was still always pretty huge." Lydia saw a connection between CLI and this need for schoolwide improvement. She suggested that a group of Cedar Bridge teachers and administrators attend a district-sponsored CLI seminar, which they did. From the outset, the approach was to involve capable and well-respected teachers and administrators in learning about CLI. This group was charged with learning about the CLI approach to teaching and determining if it would be a good fit for Cedar Bridge.

Seymore recalled that "some of our language arts teachers and more veteran teachers came back [from the CLI workshop] and said this is kind of like what we need . . . [It is] probably a piece that we are missing at our school." Although the school had invested heavily in reading instruction, teachers and administrators were concerned that they had not paid sufficient attention to the particular cultural and linguistic needs of African American and Latino students.

Cedar Bridge took the unusual step of flying a group of six teachers and administrators to visit the charter school that the founder of CLI, Jay Williams, had designed as proof of the CLI concept. This K–8 school was founded on the principles of cultural and linguistic teaching. Seymore said:

> [We were] very, very impressed with his elementary school K–5. The middle school grades, which are our grades, were not as impressive. But two things: his seventh and eighth graders had not gone to his school, because the school was new, so they kind of got new kids. . . . The kids who had been . . . there since kindergarten and first grade . . . were very impressive. [And] there were still strategies and techniques . . . that we could use and also some philosophy stuff that we could take from his [school]; even what they were doing in elementary school, [we could apply to] . . . our own practices here.

Seymore described two criteria that helped determine whether the CLI instructional resource should be made available to teachers at Cedar Bridge: (1) the extent to which the instructional approach cohered with Cedar Bridge's conception of teaching and learning and (2) whether or not the aim of CLI met a perceived need at Cedar Bridge.

Seymore and the school delegation determined that "if we want to reach our ultimate goal, which is . . . reducing the achievement gap between African American and Latino kids . . . it needs to be done through recognition of strategies and styles that fit our African American cultures and Latino cultures." The decision was carefully considered by the delegation, many of whom would be the users of the CLI instructional technology.

The intentional way Cedar Bridge gathered information about CLI before deciding to invest in it helped the school plan for its introduction and use. When Cedar Bridge staff decided they "want[ed] to have CLI professional development opportunities here at the site," they already knew a great deal about the approach and its underlying theories of learning. Before selecting this instructional technology, they were confident that it was a good fit with students' learning needs and the school's instructional philosophy. Vetting the degree of fit between the resource and the resource users in advance made sense to Cedar Bridge leaders because implicit in the decision to adopt CLI practices was an expectation that teachers would use CLI methods in their teaching.

Selecting this instructional resource meant an equally important and reciprocal commitment by the school that it would provide a range of supports to help teachers learn how to use CLI effectively. As a result of its identification and selection process, Cedar Bridge was able to design a plan for introducing CLI to the school that administrators and teachers thought would have the greatest chance of helping teachers understand the CLI philosophy and use CLI methods with students. Teachers were asked to try some of the CLI strategies in their teaching and report back at a staff meeting about their experience. That year, all six teachers I observed at Cedar Bridge used CLI methods in their teaching to varying degrees.

Deciding to Establish Professional Learning Communities at Cedar Bridge
The approach Cedar Bridge took to select professional learning communities (PLCs) differed from the way it selected CLI in one significant way: the process was much faster. However, the approach still involved some initial scouting, a rationale for how PLCs would help Cedar Bridge improve teaching and learning, and a teacher/administrative team that functioned as a sounding board for the design of the PLC implementation.

When Seymore Everett and his assistant principal, RJ Bookman, attended a four-day DuFour conference about PLCs, PLCs were still a relatively new organizational form in schools. The PLC structure appealed to Seymore because he thought that its purpose was fundamentally different from the structures and approaches to collaboration currently used at Cedar Bridge. Seymore understood the PLC structure and concept this way:

> Some people are using PLC . . . as another name for collaboration, but there are some drastic differences which make PLCs different than just collaborating, and it's the structure of the PLCs that is so important to know and to learn and to experience. [It is different from] our normal kind of collaboration: let's meet and discuss what we're going to teach tomorrow or next week or next month. . . . Therefore, [providing] . . . training . . . about how to run an effective PLC [is imperative]. I think [it] is critical for people to understand what . . . an actual functioning PLC looks like. As opposed to just let's change the name of collaborating to do our lesson plan to . . . a PLC. Our assistant principal, RJ Bookman, and I were fortunate enough to go to a four-day PD training at the end of August a week before our retreat, and in those four days, we got a lot of useful information about the purpose, the structure of PLCs.

The PLC purpose and participation structure, as Seymore understood it, was different from the way teachers currently collaborated at Cedar Bridge. The PLC was intended to examine student learning, which was a different activity from planning lessons. As in many schools, lesson planning was the "normal kind of collaboration" at Cedar Bridge. Indeed, learning about PLCs revealed a need at Cedar Bridge for a different kind of teacher collaboration.

As Seymore and his assistant principal made sense of PLCs in the context of Cedar Bridge and its needs, they knew that they needed to show how the form and function of a PLC was different from the way that teachers currently collaborated in their grade-level and department meetings. As Seymore and RJ considered the potential value of the PLC structure, they thought hard about how PLCs were different from the collaborative structures already in place at Cedar Bridge, and what a PLC would enable teachers to do in their daily work.

Part of their sense-making process involved presenting the PLC concept to the school leadership team, composed of administrators and teachers, during their August retreat. At this meeting, Seymore described an institutional need at Cedar Bridge that he thought the PLC structure filled: "We still need to figure out how to provide meaningful instruction to students and to provide formative assessments so that we can figure out if students are learning what we're teaching. I want teachers here to be doing more of this [figuring out how to provide meaningful instruction]." Months later, Lydia thought back and described how Seymore and the assistant principal had introduced the organizational structure of the PLC to the leadership team:

> They told the leadership team, basically the department chairs, about it for about forty-five minutes or an hour at the retreat. . . . Then we just all . . . started trying to do it [PLCs] and we put aside all the professional development time that we had built into the schedule; all of that [became] training people how to work in PLCs and shifting to looking at the [student] work, discussing it and being kind of systematic about it.

"Training people how to work in PLCs" became an intentional learning focus at Cedar Bridge. This focus explains many subsequent decisions that Cedar Bridge made in the design and execution of their PLC meetings.

The rationale Seymore and RJ presented for trying the PLC structure had resonated with the school leadership group. Lydia said that she and probably several other teachers had wanted to look at student work before, but "without it being required from Seymore . . . it would be the last thing to happen." Again, we see that the decision to select and begin using an instructional resource occurred when the purpose of the resource (the PLC) cohered with educators' beliefs about teaching and learning. We also see that a cross-role team of administrators and teachers was consulted before the principal decided to introduce PLCs to the staff. The manner in which Cedar Bridge did this involved "training people how to work in PLCs." From the outset, Cedar Bridge leaders structured and supported a particular sort of participation in the PLC process.

Once the leadership team members agreed to the PLC idea, they continued to work together until November to identify and design the particular aspects of PLCs that would be necessary to make this structure was a meaningful organizational resource for Cedar Bridge. The time Cedar Bridge invested in collectively designing and planning how teachers would work within the context of their PLCs so that particular adult learning needs in the school were addressed was a hallmark of their ultimate success—and also a unique characteristic of Cedar Bridge's approach to introducing instructional resources into the school.[6]

Fitting PLCs to the Adult Learning Needs at Cedar Bridge

By October, Seymore was able to articulate his vision for how the PLC structure would overcome a shortcoming he saw in the school's existing weekly grade-level and subject area meetings. Seymore wanted teachers to focus on evidence of student learning.

> We want to make that shift more to, what are kids learning? Because a lot of times when we're collaborating, we'll plan this unit—what strategies are we going to use, what standards are we going to cover, what techniques are we going to use, what kind of group work are we going to use, what kind of activity? Again, that's more centered around what *we are doing as teachers*. Where we want to start moving this towards is: *what are kids learning* and, [to that end], evaluating student work.

Seymore's interest in and conception of PLCs was as an organizational structure to guide and aid instructional improvement. He connected the PLC structure to a particular need with regard to teacher collaboration. Seymore had a clear learning goal in mind for the teachers, which was rooted in knowledge of how the teachers currently collaborated with each other.

Figure 4.1 maps Seymore's clear learning goal for using PLCs on the resource use spectrum and anticipates that his use of PLCs has the potential to deepen his understanding of teachers' learning needs and lead to the development of improved instruction for Cedar Bridge students. As he connected the PLC structure to this particular problem, it shaped the way in which Seymore worked with his colleagues and ultimately introduced PLCs to Cedar Bridge teachers. In turn, the manner in which PLCs were

FIGURE 4.1 *Seymore's learning goal on the resource use spectrum*

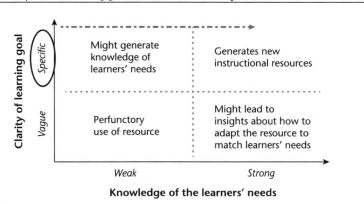

introduced influenced how the staff responded to and participated in this new structure. When instructional resources are well fitted to an instructional context, they are more likely to be used. However, as with Molly's use of talking-to-the-text in her classroom, fitting the use of a resource to the particular needs of the learners requires ongoing adjustments and paying close attention to how well the design and use of that resource are achieving the intended learning goals. Being well attuned to one's existing instructional resources can help fit the use of a specific resource to a particular context. Conducting a quick inventory of the existing instructional resources can be a useful way to scan the current environment for its instructional assets.

Conducting an Instructional Resource Inventory An instructional resource inventory is a quick way to identify the four types of instructional resources that are available within a setting as well as any critical resources needed to accomplish the learning goal. Table 4.4 shows a simple structure for taking stock of the four types of instructional resources that are available to a particular school or grade-level or subject-area team. Such inventories are most useful when conducted with a specific learning goal in mind. The table calls out available resources and resources that will need to be developed or acquired.

TABLE 4.4 *Instructional resource inventory*

	EXISTING RESOURCES	NEEDED RESOURCES
Instructional knowledge		
Instructional relationships		
Instructional technology: Tools, materials, and methods		
Organizational roles and routines		

We can imagine that if the Humanities Department at Cedar Bridge had completed such an instructional resource inventory when it began to focus on improving the academic performance of its African American and Latino students, that inventory might look like table 4.5.

Aided in part by hindsight, this instructional resource inventory reveals that although Cedar Bridge had put quite a few organizational structures in place to support teacher collaboration and joint work on instruction, these structures served more to support planning activities among teachers than to assess the quality and extent of what students were learning. For instance, Seymore realized that the collaboration time did not provide participation structures that required teachers to examine evidence of student learning or discuss what the evidence revealed about students' understanding. Nor did the structures even require teachers to look together at various aspects of their instructional practice. Recognizing that a different type of teacher participation would be needed if PLCs were to foster these sorts of instructional relationships, Cedar Bridge intentionally designed its PLCs to structure a specific type of interaction among participants. Teachers collectively examined samples of student work and used their joint analysis to design instructional next steps.

TABLE 4.5   *Hypothetical instructional resource inventory for Cedar Bridge*

Teaching and learning goal:
Improve the academic performance of African American and Latino students

	EXISTING RESOURCES	NEEDED RESOURCES
Instructional knowledge	• Methods for teaching reading to adolescents • Content knowledge—grade-appropriate literary texts for teaching, writer's workshop knowledge; knowledge of ELA standards	• Culturally responsive pedagogies • Linguistic backgrounds of African American students
Instructional relationships	• Respect for veteran colleagues' knowledge of RA methods and teaching knowledge • Trusting friendships between some teachers and between some teachers and the instructional coach	• Trust between the new teachers who were hired and rest of the humanities teachers • Collegial conversations about teaching and learning, especially involving an entire grade-level team • Discussion of teaching practices
Instructional technology: Tools, materials, and methods	• RA tools: reading inventories, talking-to-text, QAR • Course curricula and grade-level projects (e.g., eighth-grade biography study) • Common instructional routines (e.g., Cornell notes) and texts • Common writing assessment prompts and rubrics	• Common formative assessments • Methods to help struggling students
Organizational roles and routines	• Staff, department, and grade-level/subject meetings • Instructional coach, department chairs • Leadership team and teachers in leadership roles	• Routines and structures in which teachers regularly and collectively examine student work for evidence of learning • Examples of what counts as evidence that shows students have achieved particular standards

Using PLCs at Cedar Bridge   From the first PLC meeting, teachers were organized into their grade-level, subject-area teaching teams. All teams met together in the library. Each small team of approximately three teachers became a PLC group. At the first Monday meeting, Seymore described the sequence of tasks that teachers would follow in the first PLC cycle. Each cycle lasted between one and two weeks. Seymore outlined the sequence of activities:

> This is what we'll need by the end of the week. Each PLC group will need to have a common lesson that they'll teach next week, and come up with a common rubric or scoring guide of how you are going to evaluate the students' performance on that lesson so that when you come together next Thursday, there can be a dialogue about how well the students learned, and can we move on.

Seymore also made the point that the lesson should be relevant and meaningful for teachers.

During the first cycle, teachers were provided with the results from the district benchmark tests given early in the school year. Teachers were asked to examine this data to identify a common student misunderstanding and together design a lesson to address this gap. Seymore said, "We're going to have an opportunity to look today at your students' scores. Knowing what's coming up in the next week or so, how can you use these lessons to address the student weaknesses that get identified?" As teachers looked at students' standardized test data for patterns or trends and mined these for instructional implications, they began to question the instructional value of this data—especially at this point in the school year. Teachers—especially the veteran teachers—balked because this information was months old and did not seem particularly relevant to their classroom teaching now. The test's focus on discrete knowledge, like grammar, and not on higher-order thinking skills, such as how to construct an analytic argument, also troubled them.

Adhering to the data analysis task, the eighth-grade humanities team found that students needed to work on "language conventions." One teacher suggested that they design a lesson on sentence structure. Another responded, "I think it depends on what we want out of this. What is *our* goal? It is *supposed* to be useful to kids. Doing something on parallelism would be discrete and easy. How well it would serve kids, I am not sure." In this teacher exchange, we hear them challenge the purpose and value of their task. Teachers were frustrated and some were quite vocal.

On the surface, the introduction of PLCs to the Cedar Bridge teachers appeared unsuccessful. However, the experience was instructive. Seymore and Lydia used the information that they gathered to deepen their understanding of what Cedar Bridge teachers needed and made adjustments to the PLC design.

Using PLCs to Help Teachers Respond to Authentic Problems of Teaching and Learning In the first PLC meeting it became clear that using standardized benchmark data to guide and improve instruction did not fit with the teachers' instructional needs. This was an instance of using available data, rather than appropriate data.[7] Seymore, Lydia, and other members of the administrative team were alert to this problem. The eighth-grade team particularly struggled with the task because they saw a disjunction between what the district test assessed and the content that they were trying to teach.

This initial experience showed Seymore and others that the district benchmark data was not useful for their purposes. At the end of the year, Seymore looked back and described this moment in the PLC process as a "turning point."

> I especially remember the eighth-grade language arts team, but all the teams [felt] . . . this was two months' worth of information. How the hell am I supposed to decide . . . [when] there's many different things the kids need. . . . Some people kept saying, . . . "I'm getting this information now in November and if I had known it back in September, I could have done something about it, but . . . it's not realistic, . . . it's not meaningful . . . to go back." . . . We started looking into formative assessments because people were realizing . . . we're waiting for these district benchmarks or the state test . . . They're summative; it's way too much information; it's too late. I need something . . . from the lesson I taught today so if I need to go back, I can. . . . That was a key piece this year . . . of how important a formative assessment can be, and it doesn't have to be something complicated. . . . It could be an . . . academic paragraph, . . . it could be an observation where kids do stuff on the whiteboard. . . . I think that was a big "ah-hah."

Confronted with the realization that the benchmark data did not fit their intended purpose for designing joint assessments in the first place, the PLC leadership team, led by Lydia, decided to focus teachers' attention on student classroom work, which would better fit teachers' instructional goals. At Cedar Bridge, a different type of student learning data was identified and recognized as more-relevant evidence of student understanding.

LESSONS LEARNED FROM PUTTING AN ORGANIZATIONAL STRUCTURE INTO USE

Because the leadership team at Cedar Bridge had a clear purpose in mind for its use of the PLC structure, they quickly recognized that the way the PLC structure was initially introduced was not going to achieve the desired learning purpose. Often, a clear learning goal is absent when an organizational structure or new practice is introduced to a setting, which makes it more difficult to evaluate the effectiveness of the change as well as to determine if adjustments are necessary.

Clear Learning Goals Aid Meaningful Resource Use

This example of how Cedar Bridge used PLCs is instructive in several respects. First of all, it is worth noting that even with all of the thoughtful sense making, distributed leadership, and preparation, the initial use of the PLCs did not turn out exactly as desired. Teachers were upset and questioned the purpose. Missteps and imperfect experiences are typical with any change; this is essential to remember. Normalizing the range of feelings that result when trying out something new is also important. In the case of Cedar Bridge, it is equally important to recognize the role that advance preparation played, especially to clarify the potential value of the PLC structure. Given their thoughtful and collective sense making about PLCs, Seymore and his leadership team were quickly able to see that the specific task they had given teachers—to analyze standardized test data on a district benchmark assessment—was not well suited to their ultimate purpose for introducing PLCs, which was to engage teachers in specific conversations about what students were learning through daily instruction.

The Learner Is Not the Problem

Seymore and the leadership team wanted teachers to develop their skills of looking for evidence of what students were actually learning from daily instruction. Based on that analysis, they wanted teachers to develop instructional next steps to help students who had not yet fully learned the skills and content taught. Because Seymore and the leadership team had a clear sense of their learning goal for teachers and the purpose for introducing PLCs, they were readily able to recognize the staff's frustration and disgruntled response to their initial PLC experience as a problem with the learning design of their PLCs. The leadership team did not conclude that the problem was the teachers' attitudes or the idea of PLCs.

In the frame of instructional capacity building, Cedar Bridge had created a new context for teacher learning—PLC meeting time. This context had a clear learning purpose, intentional selection of participants, and an activity structure that was aligned and iteratively fitted to the overall learning purpose. The PLC activity structure involved collectively looking at evidence of student learning to design lesson instruction, then teaching that lesson and bringing back evidence of student learning for close inspection. However, the original content of the PLC meeting— standardized test score data—did not quite match the intended purpose for these meetings.

Using Instructional Resources Purposefully Can Generate More Instructional Resources

Analysis of this example shows how putting an instructional resource to use can begin an iterative process of considering how well the particular use of that resource (here, the PLC structure) is achieving the overall learning purpose. Invariably, the process of scrutinizing the use and effects of an instructional resource can reveal places where adjustments are needed. Making these iterative adjustments and adaptations is the process of *fitting* an instructional resource to the dimensions of the context. Key aspects of the fitting process are represented on the resource use spectrum (shown in figure 2.2), with each quadrant representing different attributes and outcomes of resource use.

Fitting a resource to meet the needs of the context of course requires using the resource. Assessing how well a resource fits the intended purpose often requires drawing upon (or possibly generating) the other types of instructional resources. In the example of using PLCs at Cedar Bridge, trusting relationships, instructional knowledge, and teachers' knowledge of instructional technology (especially standardized tests) were each drawn upon to determine that the use of standardized test data was problematic. And, each of these resources helped shape the adjustments that Cedar Bridge made to future PLC meetings so that they could better achieve the defined learning goals. The modifications to the PLC design were actually informed by an array of available instructional resources.

Through this fitting process, which occurred iteratively over the course of the school year, other instructional resources were also created. Teachers developed a shared repertoire of instructional practice with demonstrated evidence of student learning; teachers' instructional relationships evolved and deepened; practices and routines for examining each other's student work and discussing evidence of student learning were developed; and administrators developed routines for providing teachers with clear and pointed feedback on how they followed up on students' misunderstandings or incomplete learning.[8] Cedar Bridge is an example of how over time having a clear goal for the use of the organizational resource (PLCs) (step 1 in figure 4.2) led to observations that teachers needed different data about student learning in order to have conversations during their PLC meetings that focused on the close relationship between teaching and student performance (step 2 in figure 4.2). These realizations then led to the ongoing creation of other instructional resources (step 3 in figure 4.2), such as creating different types of common student performance data to analyze during PLCs and developing feedback routines for the teachers regarding their analyses of student work and the instructional next steps that they developed. Ultimately, this intentional use of an instructional resource (an organizational structure), fitted to the four learning dimensions within the context of Cedar Bridge, helped the school to grow its instructional capacity, as depicted in figure 4.2.

FIGURE 4.2 *Use of PLCs at Cedar Bridge as mapped on the resource use spectrum*

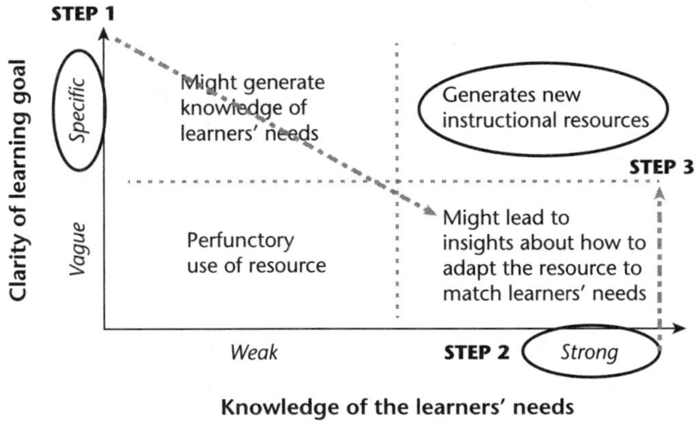

The Principal Plays a Critical Role in the Introduction and Use of Organizational Structures to Improve Instruction
=====

At Cedar Bridge, the use of PLCs sustained, evolved, and deepened over the course of the year. The vignette in chapter 1 offers one image of how meaningful and instructive some of the PLC conversations were. However, we can also imagine that under different circumstances, the initial and unwelcome introduction of PLCs might have been sufficient reason for other school leaders to abandon the PLC idea completely or to abdicate leadership responsibility and let teachers decide how to use that time. Seymore did not do this because he was clear about what he wanted teachers to learn through their participation in PLCs. He also thought there was an important role for leaders to play in structuring a conversation about student learning and its relationship to specific instructional practices. On the resource use spectrum (figure 4.2), Seymore's clear learning goal for teachers led to a better understanding of what teachers needed to learn in order to examine the relationship between their instruction and students' learning. This learning trajectory of the leadership team led to the creation of various additional instructional resources and increased the school's overall capacity for instructional improvement.

THE LEARNING ENVIRONMENT AT LIBERTY MIDDLE SCHOOL

At Liberty Middle School, Principal Lee Hoff had a different view of the role of principal and a less developed understanding of teacher collaboration. This led to a different instantiation of the PLC model as well as a distinct approach to how instructional resources were identified, introduced, and ultimately put into use in the school.

Liberty Middle School served a diverse group of seven hundred students. The two largest student groups in the school were Asian (37%) and African American (31%), constituting 68% of the student body. As table 4.1 shows, many students (60%) were eligible for free and/or reduced-price lunch. Teacher turnover was relatively high; the average number of years of teaching experience at Liberty was 4.5 years, as compared to 7.9 years at Cedar Bridge.

At Liberty, I followed the work of two English language arts (ELA) teams and one history team. Across these three teams, only two teachers (Pat and Sue) had taught for more than two years. Of these two, only one, Sue, had taught at Liberty for more than two years. She was now in her third year at the school and was the chair of the English Department. Three of the teachers were in their second year of teaching and one was a first-year teacher. (See table 4.6 for a summary of the case study participants.) Half

TABLE 4.6 *Liberty case study participants*

NAME	ROLE	YEARS AT LIBERTY
Lee Hoff[b]	Principal	5
Rae Cobb	Assistant principal	4
Will[a]	6th-grade history teacher	2
Pat[a]	6th-grade history teacher	2
Kay[a]	6th-grade history teacher	2
Fran	8th-grade English teacher	1
Sue	8th-grade English teacher	3
Meg[a]	8th-grade English teacher	2

Note: Liberty pseudonyms are one-syllable names.
[a] Denotes RA participants at the time of the study.
[b] Denotes previous RA participation.

of these teachers had entered the profession through Teach for America (TFA). The inexperience of the humanities staff at Liberty is typical of many urban schools that serve high poverty and predominantly minority student populations. By comparison, the humanities teachers at Cedar Bridge were quite experienced, with only one first-year teacher (Molly) and one third-year teacher who was new to the school (Maisey).

Principal Lee Hoff had been the principal at Liberty for five years; this was her first job as principal. When Lee came to Liberty, she stepped into a challenging situation in which to grow instructional capacity. She described her introduction to the school this way:

> I didn't know anything about [Liberty]. The superintendent was get-
> ting the boot at the moment he appointed me and dethroned the
> prior principal. . . . I came [to visit] and the principal . . . wouldn't
> talk to me. Didn't help me. Didn't give me keys. Did nothing. And
> so I had to wait until July 1 when [the school] was technically mine,
> and then I got to come here and try to figure out what was going on,
> which was really difficult, and it was just a disaster in my mind. . . .
> There were just no really good systems. It was not about the kids first.
> There wasn't a real cohesive-like thing. There was no real vision for
> what the kids should be able to do. . . . It was just a mess and so I
> just wanted to fix it. . . . To me, that just meant . . . trying to get us
> all going in the same direction. . . . It was a difficult situation, but it's
> difficult in a lot of schools in this district and . . . you have people
> who have a real hard time with the cultures that the kids bring. The
> kids don't always bring . . . a happy, let's-learn attitude. . . . There's
> just a lot of challenges. And so, people who really didn't want to
> kind of revisit what we were doing and change how we were being
> responsive to the kids, they decided to go elsewhere. And people who
> wanted to try and . . . look at . . . academic excellence for all were
> people who stayed.

In her first year at Liberty, Lee made changes to the instructional staff and created organizational structures intended to support teachers' professional development.

Lee's concern for putting the "kids first" stands out. The first time I met her she was on her way out to the playground to play kickball with the kids. She'd just had a conversation with a teacher in which she asked him to explain and justify his grading system. "What is the grade a reflection of?" she asked. When his response was mastery of the material, she asked, "What grade reflects mastery? What if students do all the work but they still don't understand? What grade does that deserve?" She wanted this teacher to see that giving a failing grade neither acknowledged the work that the student may have done nor offered encouragement to continue to study and work.

Lee's sixteen years of combined teaching and administrative experience shaped her beliefs: about the need for developmentally appropriate instruction; about learning, which for her fundamentally required developing an amicable relationship with the learner; about the need for schools to be reorganized so that teachers were less isolated from each other; and about the principal's role, which in her mind was largely to stay out of the teachers' way and let them "do their job." Lee explained that in her five years she had tried to get teachers at Liberty to "revisit what we were doing and change how we were being responsive to the kids."

Lee said that when she arrived at Liberty, only 5 percent of the African American students were scoring at the proficient level on the standardized tests, which was a smaller proportion of students than the special education population. She was proud that Liberty's test scores had improved considerably during her tenure as principal. She wanted to "give people an excellent public education" and for her, doing so required some combination of "developmental responsiveness and social equity." As she sought to move the teachers at Liberty toward her vision, she grew to believe that hiring teachers with similar goals was key. She often said that the staff and their beliefs was critical: "It's like the bus is going in this direction. If people don't want to go in that direction, it's very hard to get the bus moving." She was eager to see some teachers go and welcomed the opportunity to hire new teachers who shared a desire to educate these students.

Teaching Is Perceived as an Individual Endeavor

Lee believed in teachers' knowledge and their abilities to make decisions. She said, "They are running the ship in that particular way. They should and if they can't, . . . they're not going to work here. They have to want to work together and figure it out." She thought it was important for teachers to work together, but she didn't have a specific vision of what that ought to look like or how teachers would need to be supported or taught how to work together in a particular manner.

Lee's big idea was that it was important to reduce the isolation that teachers often experience on the job. She recounted her own isolation as a high school science teacher:

"I've tried to make Liberty a place where [teachers] have support from each other, which is really important so their day isn't like my days were—I would get to school an hour early to get in the Xerox line so I could get something copied. Then I just went to my room and I didn't see anybody except maybe at lunch if someone wandered into my room, because I didn't go to the lunchroom."

She wanted teachers to receive support from one another, but she did not specify what that support would look like. In the words of one teacher, "[Liberty] has a very high level of coordination in terms of teachers collaborating with each other." That coordination was reflected in Lee's commitment to make sure each teaching pair had time to meet together each week during the school day. She hired substitutes to pay for teachers' release time each week because their individually scheduled planning periods did not necessarily match up with their teaching partner's.

Lee's past experience as a science high school teacher had taught her that it is not effective to require teachers to use a particular strategy. "'Oh, you need to learn this.' You know, that's just not effective. I know because I've tried it. I'm not speaking theoretically here. I'm speaking *absolutely* that it's not effective."

Lee didn't believe in a silver-bullet, "if everybody did this, we'd all be proficient" approach. Certain in her beliefs that there were many effective ways to teach and that she could not force teachers to learn anything in particular, she allowed and even encouraged teacher-directed, autonomous decision making about instructional practice. Unlike at Cedar Bridge, where Seymore also valued teachers' knowledge, Lee did not have a vision of what teachers learning from their instructional practice together could look like.

When teachers serendipitously adopted the same instructional method, she recognized there was value in having a common instructional approach. In a story about how Step Up to Writing became the way "all the language arts teachers are now [teaching writing] because it's what we do" at Liberty, she describes the accidental manner in which the program was adopted. She said one TFA-trained teacher used the Step Up to Writing approach and "shared with some of the people here in the department, and they were like, 'Oh, wow, this is really cool.'" Lee said that as other TFA teachers who were also familiar with Step Up to Writing arrived at Liberty, the method caught on. She noted: "The nice thing about it is that other teachers can use it. . . . It gives kids a consistent format and they repeat it over and over again, which has been . . . very powerful."

Although she saw the value for students when teachers used the same instructional method, she did not mention ways in which this might help teachers to strengthen or refine their teaching. She did not promote common instructional approaches as Cedar Bridge did. Nor did Lee seem to think that she needed to guide teachers to have conversations about how they were actually teaching. Consequently, Liberty teachers approached instruction in quite different ways, even if they used the same instructional technology. At the end of the year when ELA teachers were asked to construct a department curriculum binder, teachers' different beliefs were exposed.

Meg: I like the idea of having a couple of questions per standard— a set of sample questions. So having the standard, the unit, and questions.

Kay: Should your assessments be like the standardized test?

Cheryl: No. My assessments are more authentic. I would not teach that way.

As reflected in teachers' different beliefs and approaches to assessment, Lee ascribed to the belief that "there's a lot of really great [instructional] strategies out there and a lot of really positive . . . things that work." She accepted "anything that's research-based and makes sense and is powerful." The variation in instructional approaches at Liberty revealed an underlying conception of teaching as an individual endeavor, rather than a shared enterprise. Lee's conception of teaching, then, differed in a profound way from that at Cedar Bridge, where excellent teaching was believed to derive from a shared set of practices that were tied to coconstructed learning goals. The belief at Cedar Bridge was that teaching ought to be continuously and collaboratively examined and refined. At Liberty, teachers' individual autonomy to make instructional decisions meant that there was no authentic reason for teachers to collaborate with each other, particularly if they had different views about teaching and learning.

Principal Beliefs Shape the Identification and Use of Instructional Resources

As part of Lee's belief that many great instructional strategies exist, she was on the lookout for other instructional technologies that might be of use to Liberty teachers. In the year I spent at Liberty, Lee identified at least a dozen different instructional technology resources that she brought to the teachers. These came in the form of professional development programs to attend, tools to try, and materials or instructional methods to use. See table 4.7 for a list of the programs that were introduced to the humanities teachers during that year.

The resources listed have different underlying conceptions of how learning occurs. For example, Accelerated Reader is a computer-based reading assessment tool; it provides a databank of multiple-choice questions on a wide range of middle school literature. Liberty teachers used it to monitor students' independent reading. Accelerated Reader provides an experience where students are asked to find the "correct" answers to standard questions, whereas talking-to-the-text, for example, gives students the experience of formulating opinions, asking questions, and making observations about what they read. The "software" of these two instructional technologies differs in significant ways.

TABLE 4.7 *Instructional resources identified by Principal Lee Hoff*

PROFESSIONAL DEVELOPMENT RESOURCE	WHEN INTRODUCED	WHO ATTENDED
Behavior Management Model	Previous year and continued	All staff
Reading Apprenticeship (RA)	August – April (7 RA sessions)	Cohort of 4 teachers attended 6 sessions
PLC Conference (DuFour)	Summer	Principal with teacher cohort
Collaborative learning teams model	August staff retreat	All staff
Cultural Linguist Instruction, Part 1	August staff retreat	All staff
Understanding by Design	September	All staff
Cultural Linguist Instruction, Part 2	October	Half of faculty attended
Edusoft	Fall	All staff
ALS benchmark tests	Fall	All staff
Accelerated Reader	January	English Department
My Access	Fall	English Department
ThinkLink	Fall	All staff
Learning Study Groups ASCD kit	Spring	All staff
Motivation workshop	Spring	Interested faculty; 12 teachers attended
Yoga/meditation approach	Spring	Interested faculty

At Cedar Bridge, an instructional technology was selected with an understanding of its "software" (i.e., information base and conception of how learning occurs) and its compatibility with Cedar Bridge's views about how students best learn. It was also introduced gradually and with a range of supports. At Liberty, Lee Hoff's approach was to introduce many resources and let the teachers figure out which were useful to them. As she put it. "I try to keep my hands out of the details as much as possible. If I see things that aren't making sense, I may ask questions: 'Well, what about this? Or, how would you deal with that?'" Ultimately, Lee viewed the principal's role as the finder and provider of instructional resources.

In addition, Lee didn't see it as her job to structure experiences whereby teachers could make sense of these resources or their effects on teaching and learning. The result was that teachers were largely on their own to evaluate this vast array of different resources, to decide if any were useful, and in what way. Nor did Lee see it as her job to structure teachers' participation during their collaborative time. She went to great lengths to provide this common time, but it was her view that teachers would best know how to use it.

Lee's view that teachers would know how to use collaboration time meaningfully presumed teachers had a great deal of knowledge: sufficient knowledge of pedagogy and content as well as knowledge of how to engage in joint work such that conflicts could be addressed constructively. It presumed that teachers would have shared instructional goals for their students and that colleagues would ask each other probing questions to get at the heart of the relationship between teaching and learning, so that students' interests would be well served. Since most humanities teachers at Liberty were relatively inexperienced, they did not have all of this instructional knowledge nor did they have knowledge of routines and practices to collaboratively and productively examine their teaching—even if they had wanted to do so.

In the absence of a shared approach to instruction at Liberty and without specific practices and routines to guide collective inquiry into the relationship between teaching and learning, teachers' individual views about what counted as evidence of student learning and how students learned best were prominent. Perhaps because the teachers I observed were relatively new to teaching, their instructional knowledge seemed strongly influenced by their preparation for teaching. The differences between teachers' preparation, and consequently their ideas about how learning occurs, were vast. Eighth-grade English teachers Meg and Sue epitomize the significant differences among the teachers I observed at Liberty.

Meg and Sue

Meg was in her second year of teaching. She had joined the Teach for America program when she graduated from college, and landed at Liberty. Sue had completed a master's degree in education and student taught for a year before entering the profession. She was only in her third year of teaching, but was the veteran teacher in the English Department and held the position of department chair. Both Meg and Sue had taught seventh-grade English the preceding year. This year they decided to "loop" with their students into the eighth grade.

Each teacher held a particular view about literacy and how learning occurs. Their views were shaped, in part, by their educational backgrounds and their preparation for the teaching profession. Meg's formal preparation for a teaching career was a month-long intensive summer institute sponsored by Teach for America. TFA looks for "exceptional individuals who have a track record of achievement in school, work, and/or extracurricular activities" and holds the "relentless pursuit of measurable results" as a core value.[9] Meg described herself as "the type of person that will put a lot of pressure on myself." She measured her own success as a teacher in terms of her students' standardized test scores:

> There was instantly a pressure when I came here to . . . perform and get my students to raise their state scores. I ended up having a really successful year and now that puts even more pressure because this year it's like I have to up . . . one-up what I did last year, which was really big.

Meg viewed her instructional role as preparing her students for the May state test and for high school. Unlike Sue, Meg was more comfortable relying on objective measures, like standardized test scores, to assess her students' learning.

Sue followed a traditional route into teaching; she received a master's degree in teaching from a local university, which required she spend a year as an apprentice teacher. Sue's ideas about education "came from her local Writer's Project and constructivism." She had a strong view that her role as English teacher was to develop students' abilities to interpret and make sense of text:

> So my idea kind of comes from how I was educated which is that, you know, we're training children to be independent readers who make their own meaning of texts, and the way they should do that is by

learning some mental strategies to do as they read. You know, making connections, making predictions, asking questions, engaging with the text.

Sue structured her eighth-grade language arts class as a series of opportunities for students to practice reading texts analytically by using a variety of methods, including questioning and predicting. Her aim was to develop a community of readers in her classroom who were able to analyze and interpret texts independently.

LESSONS LEARNED FROM LIBERTY

The manner in which instructional resources were identified and then used at Liberty offers instructive lessons about the important role the principal has in shaping a school's culture of learning. The principal's beliefs about how adults learn shape the conditions for learning that the principal creates within the school. In addition, the examples of the PLC meetings at Liberty, when juxtaposed with those at Cedar Bridge, demonstrate that teachers need to be shown how to use collaborative time to learn together and from their teaching.

Providing Meeting Time Does Not Ensure Collaboration

Lee provided a weekly prep period when each grade-level subject-area teaching team could collaborate during the school day. She hired substitutes to make these team meetings possible. In the year I spent at Liberty, teaching pairs met routinely and reported valuing this time to work together. Some teachers, however, thought the depth of collaboration was limited. According to Will, "The administration pushes it orally at least, like they talk about that it's really important to collaborate . . . [but] not a lot of people [act collaboratively]." The reason some teachers found the depth of collaboration lacking is that meaningful collaboration—where participants learn together and challenge each other's thinking and assumptions—does not automatically occur just because teachers meet. Shallow collaboration, characterized by minimal teacher learning, is not a structural problem but rather a cultural one.

Providing time for teachers to meet may be an important step toward making meaningful collaboration possible. It certainly is a way to reduce the extreme degree of isolation that Lee described experiencing when she worked as a high school teacher. However, meaningful collaboration where teachers jointly inspect students' work—as well as their own and their colleagues'—for evidence of learning and trace this learning back to their instructional decisions, and where teachers routinely ask questions of themselves and their practice, requires more than time. It requires having routines and sociocultural practices that guide teachers' interactions to develop shared instructional knowledge, instructional repertoires, and the capacity to identify and use appropriate instructional technology. In other words, such organizational routines and practices tied to achieving common learning goals will cultivate strong instructional relationships among educators that in turn will continue to build an organization's instructional capacity.

A Structural Solution Won't Solve a Cultural Problem

As Dan Lortie documented in his sociological study of the schoolteacher, historically, "schools were organized around teacher separation rather than teacher interdependence."[10] This is still largely how teaching is practiced in schools today. This means that organizing meaningful collaboration and collective learning among teachers that aims to affect the way instruction is conducted and student learning occurs will require much more than creating structures that give teachers time to work together.

At Liberty, the well-meaning solution to increase collaboration among pairs of subject and grade-level teachers did not go far enough to provide a vision for how to use this time productively nor was there enough of an attempt to structure teachers' participation. To Sue, the administration's vision of collaboration seemed limited. She recalled how it was communicated to teachers at their August retreat:

[The administrators'] big philosophy is that you will develop common assessments and then you teach in your own way and then you compare your results on the common assessment that you developed. So we kind of learned about that a little bit at the beginning of school. . . .

So it was the *pseudo* all-staff professional development, but it wasn't a real professional development. It was like the principal talked about it for twenty minutes and she was like, "We should do this because it's really great to collaborate. Okay. Moving on." And so I feel like everyone's understanding of what it means is different. . . . Like what exactly are we supposed to be doing with the collaboration?

Evidence that people's conceptions of collaboration differed was prevalent at Liberty. This is not surprising since a shared purpose for collaboration was not cultivated. With minimal communication and limited time for discussion about its purpose, the expectation for collaboration was distilled down to a single practice: develop common assessments.

Developing unit assessments that matched the form of the standardized tests students took multiple times during the year was the repeated collaborative work of the three teaching teams I followed. There was little or no evidence that teachers' coconstruction of common assessments occurred in a manner that allowed teachers to deepen their instructional or subject-matter knowledge, or to develop professional relationships with one another. For example, no teaching team used the student results from the common assessments as an opportunity to look at student work, or to discuss students' learning in terms of their instructional approaches, which varied quite considerably.

Structured Participation Enables Examination of the Teaching-Learning Relationship

Teachers' participation in these collaborative meetings, unlike at Cedar Bridge, was not structured for the teachers beyond the assigned task of developing common unit assessments. Consequently, this became the chief purpose of these meetings. Having common assessments across subject-area classrooms in a grade level might be a useful (or even necessary) structure to help teachers ask important questions about teaching and learning. With common assessments, teachers can look at student results on a common measure of learning across different classroom environments. They can ask what is being learned and by whom. Teachers can see which students in which classrooms are not learning and can look for patterns among both students and teachers. They can ask questions of one another: How did you teach this content to these students? Although creating such common assessments may cause teachers to have conversations about what they want students to learn and how they should measure that learning—both important aspects of teaching—the assessments alone do not necessarily lead to using the results of those assessments to examine the relationship between what students are learning and how they are being taught.

The leadership team at Cedar Bridge recognized that teachers' default behavior when they met together was to plan—to plan lessons, units of study, final projects. This is why the Cedar Bridge leaders wanted the PLC groups to follow a highly structured process of looking at student work for evidence of learning. They wanted to change teachers' routine behavior and practices when they came together. They wanted teachers to focus on what students were doing and learning and use their analysis of student learning as the basis from which to plan. Thus, Cedar Bridge leaders developed a specific series of steps for teachers to follow. Start with the student work. Then, collaboratively assess that work. Use their joint analysis of what students did and did not learn to design, within a day or two, instruction with a built-in formative assessment. Then, finally, a few days later, come back to look together at the results of the formative assessments. Did students' learning increase? Were the adjustments made to instruction effective, and for whom? This process, which the teacher teams engaged in five times across the school year, was highly structured. In addition, all the teachers were in the same room so teams were engaging in this process in public. Finally, at the close of the last meeting in each cycle, there was a quick, but important, opportunity for sharing insights and questions across the PLC teams. Questions—such as, What did you notice your African American students were struggling with?—helped individual PLCs see connections across their subject areas and grade levels.

In a fundamental way, Principal Seymore Everett realized that teachers did not know how to engage in collaborative work with one another where the learning-teaching relationship was the centerpiece of the collaborative work. So, Cedar Bridge structured a process that adhered to three principles:

1. Place the learning-teaching relationship at the center.
2. Make the work of every PLC visible and public (by having the teams meet in the library).
3. Give teams direct feedback on the quality of their PLC work.

Although the will to improve student learning, especially for the lowest performing students, was great at Liberty, there was little collective knowledge about how best to do this. In addition, the collaborative structures that provided time for teachers to work together were not sufficiently structured to develop this collective knowledge—or even a shared conception of the particular teaching and learning challenges that Liberty teachers confronted.

SUMMARY

Chapters 3 and 4 have examined what schools can do to expand their capacity for adult learning. Schools can create opportunities for the intentional use of instructional resources. One way to do this is by designing a purposeful process for identifying and selecting instructional technology. Another helpful approach is to establish organizational structures that support the effective use of instructional technology. Such structures are most effective when some sort of continuous feedback loop is part of the design so that the users of the technology are able to inspect how well their use of a particular instructional resource is achieving the intended learning goal. The resource use spectrum was introduced as a tool to help identify why a particular use of a resource may be ineffective. It also illustrates how fitting the use of an instructional resource to a learning purpose and to the needs of the learners can generate additional instructional resources.

CHAPTER 5

HOW CAN DISTRICTS SUPPORT PRINCIPAL LEARNING?

Critical Friends Conversations and Instructional Site Visits

T his chapter considers the sorts of supports that principals need in order to lead instructional improvement and build instructional capacity in their school. I explore two questions:

1. What do principals need to know in order to lead instructional improvement?
2. How can central office administrators support principals in developing instructional capacity in their schools?

Guided by the ideas within the instructional capacity building framework, I describe how a group of district elementary school supervisors in the Coopersville Unified School District (CUSD) began to answer these questions.[1] This particular group of district administrators, referred to as DES for short, oversaw sixty elementary schools. They were responsible for overseeing the day-to-day management of the schools. Yet, as chapters 5–7 will show, this group of administrators envisioned an expanded role for themselves and forged a new way to work together to provide a different sort of support to CUSD elementary schools. The DES wanted to develop ways to help the principals they supervised grow as instructional leaders. To do so, they reimagined the purpose of principal meetings and created two structures intended to support principal learning: Critical Friends Conversations (CFCs) and instructional site visits (ISVs).

This chapter describes those structures and how they were used. Ideas from the ICB framework guide the analysis and demonstrate the extent to which the use of CFCs and ISVs created opportunities for a group of principals to grow as instructional leaders. I explore the following questions: How were the organizational structures introduced to the principals? What learning goals were these structures intended to address? What were the learners' (principals') needs? Did use of these organizational structures expand instructional capacity, and if so, how? This analysis considers the extent to which use of these structures generated additional instructional resources (i.e., knowledge, technology, relationships, and other organizational structures) as an indication of whether or not the DES developed principals' capacity to lead instructional improvement.

LEADING INSTRUCTIONAL IMPROVEMENT IN COOPERSVILLE ELEMENTARY SCHOOLS

Over the past few years, CUSD had developed a district strategic plan to improve learning outcomes for students. The plan identified several strategic priorities, including implement the district core curriculum, use student data to guide instruction, provide academic and behavioral support to schools, and differentiate the type of central office support provided to schools according to their needs. Guided by these district priorities, the DES conceived of and led efforts to strengthen principals' capacity to lead instructional improvement in their schools. A two-year study of how the DES did this from the district office examined the specific changes that the DES made to their twice-monthly elementary principal meetings. These changes were intended to help principals become effective leaders of the district priorities, including the instructional changes necessitated by new state standards.

The DES saw a need to reconfigure district-led elementary principal meetings so that principals were positioned as active learners rather than passive receivers of information. The CFCs and ISVs were the DES's attempt to organize opportunities for principals to learn about Common

Core–aligned instruction and leading instructional improvement. One veteran administrator expressed principals' learning needs this way:

> What I think is most essential right now is principals being positioned to describe the shifts in vision in the Common Core Standards and knowing them well enough to be able to inspire teachers to want to make those shifts for themselves, to look for them when they visit classrooms, and to comment on those things directly.

The focal activities within the CFC and ISV structures involved principals' identifying challenges related to improving instruction at their sites, visiting classrooms in each other's schools, and talking with one another about their leadership work. In these new formats, principals were asked to become active learners and given opportunities to shape the content of these meetings.

The Creation of Structures to Support Principal Learning

Once the DES recognized that principals needed opportunities to learn about leading instructional improvement, they realized that the principal meetings provided the time for this learning. However, they also realized the meetings needed restructuring. To do this, the DES followed four design principles, developed by a small group of elementary, middle, and high school principals and central office administrators. This group was convened by the superintendent and facilitated by a central office administrator with expertise in distributing leadership and leading professional learning. These design principles were:

1. Make the facilitation and structure of the principal meetings reflect the pedagogy we want to see in classrooms across the district.
2. Design meeting structures to elicit widespread leadership and participation.
3. Differentiate content to ensure accessibility and relevance for all.
4. Model transparent facilitation and the use of purposeful structures so that leaders can replicate these structures and practices at their sites as they design and lead meetings.

The DES drew upon these principles to develop the CFCs and ISVs. These principles communicated an expectation that the content and structure of school site leader meetings be meaningful. They also seemed to reflect the sentiment that you learn the work by doing the work rather than by being told what to do.[2] The manner in which these principles were created as well as the actual principles represented a change in district practice. The principles provided a vision of a school site leader meeting that was a significant contrast to existing elementary principal meetings, which were conducted as occasions for providing information to a captive audience.

NEW OPPORTUNITIES FOR PRINCIPAL LEARNING

The CFCs offered a designated time for monthly conversations among principals about a problem related to leading instructional improvement. The ISVs were a monthly school site visitation cycle where principals observed teaching and learning in elementary classrooms. (The ISV structure is examined in chapter 6.)

As table 5.1 outlines, these new structures were intended to create specific kinds of learning opportunities for principals and to focus principals' attention on matters related to high-quality instruction. Many members of DES emphasized the instructional focus of the new structures. One noted, "Our meeting structures used to be heavily around other topics, and so we cleared that and focused it on instruction." Another said, "If you look at the structures that we now have in place—our principal meetings, our school visits, our networks—they're around that instructional focus." A third described the goals for the district's work with principals this way:

> It's helping them [principals] build the infrastructure at the site . . . to actually reflect on their practices so that they can get better at what they do. That's much easier said than done, because the day-to-day gets in the way every day. I want to try to strip [away] some of that day-to-day so they can refocus their efforts. You can get consumed by a parent complaint or an incident that happens between the adults or an adult and a child.

TABLE 5.1 *Comparison of the two organizational structures for principal learning*

CONTEXT DIMENSIONS	CRITICAL FRIENDS CONVERSATIONS	INSTRUCTIONAL SITE VISITS
Purpose	"Examine a problem related to leading instruction and structure solutions, sometimes in the form of specific action steps, that principals could take"	"Analyze student learning under new standards; sharpen equity lens; share strategies for improving teaching and learning; develop a commitment to action"
Participants	Principals and the DES	Principals and the DES (sometimes also assistant principals, literacy coaches, and district staff with curriculum and instruction expertise)
Content		
Data used	Principal named a leadership problem; recounted a relevant situation and/or shared one or two key documents related to the problem	Participants' scripted classroom observation notes
Next steps	Presenter summary and short and long-term next steps (5 minutes)	Developed as a group for host principal/school (15 minutes)
Activity structure		
Facilitator	Principal	Two district elementary supervisors (DES)
Problem of practice	Principal-selected problem of leadership practice; usually a managerial or operational problem	Principal-selected problem of instructional practice, related to instruction and the CCSS
Time allotted	45–50 minutes	3 hours
Frequency	Monthly	Monthly
Follow-up	None	Nothing formal

Stated another way, the DES wanted to help principals build their school's capacity to improve instruction and create meaningful opportunities for students to learn. To do so, the DES focused on ways to increase the individual instructional leadership capacity of elementary principals.

The DES also wanted to invest in principals' collective instructional leadership capacity. This goal led to another purpose of these two structures, although it was not made explicit. One elementary supervisor who had previously been a principal in the district explained that another reason for creating these structures "was for principals to find a meaningful learning environment for themselves where they could have more of an opportunity to form partnerships and collectively work together to . . . implement [instructional shifts] at the school sites." Principals in Coopersville, as in many districts, worked in a solitary way. Although principals had met twice a month for years, these meetings were not designed for them to discuss their leadership approaches and challenges. Thus, most principals did not really know each other all that well as leaders, even if they were long-time colleagues in CUSD—and they knew even less about the specific leadership challenges or instructional improvements efforts under way in each other's schools.

CRITICAL FRIENDS CONVERSATIONS AS A SITE FOR PRINCIPAL LEARNING

The following discussion examines how the Critical Friends Conversations were designed and facilitated with the intent of helping principals develop as instructional leaders. The discussion also reveals shortcomings in how the CFCs were used that ultimately limited the available opportunities for principal learning.

The Activity Structure and Participant Role

Critical Friends Conversations took up a third of each monthly principal meeting. They were a deliberate attempt by the DES to create an environment within the traditional principal meeting to support principals as learners, particularly as learners of instructional leadership. The stated purpose of these discussions was to help principals examine a problem related to leading instruction in their school. During CFCs, the sixty elementary principals met in three separate rooms, each led by two elementary supervisors. Principals met in small groups of five to seven; group membership stayed the same all year. The DES used a protocol, the Document-Based Critical Friends Group Protocol, to structure the monthly conversations. It had a series of steps that principals were supposed to follow.

Critical Friends Conversation Procedures

1. Principal presents problem of practice (5–10 minutes)
2. Participants ask clarifying questions and presenter responds (5 minutes)
3. Participants write probing questions; presenter reflects out loud on questions that resonate the most (10 minutes)
4. Participants discuss solutions; presenter listens (10–15 minutes)
5. Presenter summarizes and addresses short- and long-term next steps (5 minutes)
6. Debrief of process (5 minutes)

In a monthly rotation, principals took turns assuming the specific roles of presenter, timekeeper, and facilitator.

The protocol described the stance principals were supposed to assume during the CFC:

> Critical friends are good listeners and problem solvers who help others sort out their thinking and make sound decisions. They ask provocative questions that help others define expectations and intentions, help them realize when their expectations for themselves and others are too low, and help them realize when their actions don't match their intentions.

In some CFC groups, this statement was read aloud at the start of each session as a way to remind and refocus principals on the activity. Principals took turns assuming the role of "presenting principal." The presenting principal was asked to formulate a problem of practice that met the following criteria:

- High leverage—will impact your school if addressed
- Actionable—something leaders can do to implement change
- Relevant to instructional improvement at your school

Presenting principals were told to select an authentic problem of leading instructional improvement in their school that they "would like peers to help solve."

Selecting the Content for the CFC Discussions

The content of each CFC session was heavily influenced by the particular leadership problem that the presenting principal brought. Selecting and formulating a worthwhile leadership problem became an important component of the CFC design. The type of problem mattered; it was the *learning content* of the CFC. The problem was supposed to be connected to the stated purpose for the CFC, which was to examine a "problem related to leading instruction." (See table 5.1.)

The DES recognized the importance of selecting and framing this problem. Therefore, in advance of the CFC sessions, elementary supervisors helped principals identify and formulate their problem of practice in one-on-one conversations. Recounting such conversations with principals, one supervisor said,

> In the beginning we did a lot of meetings one on one with principals. [We said,] "This is what a problem of practice is. Identify how you would like to use this time around your problem of practice, which means it's something you don't know the answer to. Don't present something that you already know, but a real question of your practice, and bring evidence of that."

Recognizing that principals were unaccustomed to being cast in the stance of a learner, the DES schooled principals in how to assume this role: Bring a "real question of your practice" and "Don't present something that you already know." In the first year of CFCs, the authenticity of the problems varied.

The opportunity to identify their own problems of practice to discuss with colleagues was a novel experience for many principals. Some appreciated this opportunity. One principal, who was not alone in her view, said, "Critical Friends is one of the best things we do." However, in the first year, many struggled to identify and name meaty problems of instructional leadership or appeared uncomfortable bringing these problems to their group.

Selecting Worthwhile Problems of Leading Instructional Improvement
Early on, the DES observed that principals needed help formulating "high-leverage problems that would affect their school if addressed." For instance, one veteran administrator commented that when he heard what one principal planned to share at a CFC meeting, he needed "to refocus him" because essentially the problem could be "distilled down to wanting to talk about a pregnant woman being angry." Another elementary supervisor reported that a "principal presented a problem of practice that was . . . a very small issue at the school with personnel . . . it was not a good use of the time." These sorts of experiences showed the DES that many principals needed to learn how to identify and frame worthwhile leadership problems.

A Solitary Approach to Leadership Work   In some ways, the DES struggled with how to help principals learn to identify and frame problems related to leading instructional improvement. They approached this process as an individual problem of principal learning rather than a collective one. Thus, each elementary supervisor worked separately with individual principals. For example, one supervisor explained, "I do a lot of work with [a principal] in advance of the Critical Friends, because I want to make sure that he is putting out there a good problem of practice that is worth everybody's time to chew on and to work through and that he has all of the right things in place." Most supervisors reported helping principals formulate their CFC problems "to make sure they're getting the best use of that hour possible." Each supervisor developed his or her own approach to this particular work.

Because the DES took a solitary approach to this leadership work, they did not discuss with one another how they approached helping principals frame leadership problems. They did not use time during principal meetings to instruct principals on how to select a worthy leadership problem or what counted as a problem of instructional leadership. Nor did the DES remind principals of the learning purpose for the CFC and revisit the importance of making sure the selected problem "related to leading instruction." There are many possible reasons why the DES approached this task individually. Whatever the reason, the isolated approach became a missed opportunity to develop principals' collective capacity for instructional leadership by honing principals' skills at identifying and framing challenges related to improving instruction.

DES Increased Their Knowledge of Principals as Instructional Leaders

The one-on-one conversations between elementary supervisors and principals, in which principals talked about their specific leadership problems, were informative for the elementary supervisors. These conversations provided an opportunity "to explore what's on [principals'] minds about a problem they have." They also helped the DES gain knowledge about principals as instructional leaders. One supervisor said, "I love the one-on-ones before [CFCs] with principals so they can be very honest with what they're trying to tackle at their schools, and then open that to others. It shows trust, risk, everything we really want to do in terms of creating an environment of learning for everyone, from kids on up to principals and leaders." Another described the conversations as "very meaningful and poignant . . . and in some cases profound, because it's just you and the principals, and they're sharing what they need help with." These conversations helped to recast the supervisory role of the elementary administrator into an educative and supportive one.

Previously, this sort of learning opportunity to discuss leadership challenges did not exist. Thus, in this example we can see how the instructional capacity building theory works. As the theory proposes, using the CFC structure in a meaningful way stimulated the creation of other instructional resources that were helpful for leading instructional improvement. For instance, elementary supervisors instituted an organizational routine in which they met with principals to discuss real leadership challenges as a way to prepare for a meaningful Critical Friends Conversation. As elementary supervisors engaged in this new routine, they developed additional knowledge of individual principals as instructional leaders and in many cases the strength of the relationship between supervisor and principal increased.

The Problem of Identifying Instructional Leadership Problems

The leadership problems that principals brought to CFC sessions in the first year were typically managerial or operational problems rather than ones aimed at improving instruction or aligning instruction to the new standards. (Less than half the problems focused directly on instructional improvement.) Midway through the first year, one elementary supervisor explained, "Originally when we were planning the Critical Friends—we even have it in writing—we wanted to focus around instruction, but . . . that's not what's happening in these meetings. [Problems center] mostly around systems in the school, professional development, climate issues, which are a huge part of running a school." One possible reason for this emphasis: CUSD principals were not accustomed to focusing their attention on matters of instruction. The typical managerial and operational problems principals initially brought to CFCs were things like "how to manage the school secretary to become a positive liaison with the parents" or "what to do about tardy students who missed important instructional time."

When principals brought forward managerial or operational problems that were "really pressing for them at their school site," the DES allowed these issues to become the focus of CFCs. But when individual supervisors were asked what they thought about principals presenting these types of problems during the CFCs, their views were divided. They began to question the original stated goal of the CFCs. One supervisor said, "We want to make this Critical Friends the principals' time to air out and flesh out some of the things that are big challenges at their school and keep them up at night." Another also thought principals needed opportunities to get help with any sort of leadership problems they faced:

Site visits are always around instruction. I don't want to take that opportunity away from the principals and say that the Critical Friends have to be around instruction, because these [managerial and operational concerns] are real things, real leadership moves that they need to make that are equally as important as instruction.

In essence, such comments suggest that these elementary supervisors thought principals would know best how to use CFCs and should be allowed to decide the focus of the conversation. This administrative decision is reminiscent of the decision the Liberty principal made under the guise of professional autonomy: teachers should decide how to use their collaborative meeting time because they know best what they need to focus on. As we saw at Liberty, this form of professional autonomy is not conducive to increasing capacity for instructional improvement nor does it boost instructional leadership capacity. In CUSD, the expected focus of the CFC was no longer how to lead instructional improvement.

In backing away from a focus on leading instructional improvement, the DES seemed unaware of the interplay among operational, managerial, and instructional leadership problems. Often, the problems presented had aspects of each, although the managerial or operational aspect was typically foregrounded. Additionally, the DES's perspective seemed to miss the opportunity to help principals frame operational or managerial problems in terms of their impact on the quality of instruction and student learning. Furthermore, this point of view failed to recognize the limitations inherent in the site visit conversations, which tended to focus on developing principals' knowledge of standards-aligned instruction rather than on actions they might take to alter teachers' instruction in their schools.

Figuring out how to focus principals' attention on actions that principals could take to alter instruction in their schools eluded the DES. One supervisor who thought that focusing CFCs specifically on problems of instructional leadership would help principals identify specific actions that they could take in their schools did not want to let go of that focus. She said DES needed to figure out if CFCs would "remain just a structure where you have a time to talk about what's important to you." Insightfully, she observed that the members of the DES "have not ever sat [together] and said, 'What are [principals] learning in these groups?'"

From an instructional capacity building perspective, the question of what the targeted learners were actually learning is important. Two other questions were important to ask: What did the DES want principals to learn from their participation in the CFCs? And was participation in the CFCs structured in a way to support that learning? These two questions undergird the resource use spectrum. Had the DES considered these questions, they might have been able to make more effective use of the CFCs to increase principals' instructional leadership capacity.

THE SPECTRUM OF RESOURCE USE AND THE CFC

Recall that the spectrum of resource use graphic considers use of a resource along two axes: the clarity of the learning goal and knowledge of the learners' needs. The DES had articulated a clear learning goal for principals with regard to the CFC: "to examine a problem related to leading instruction and to structure solutions, sometimes in the form of specific action steps, that principals could take." However, as the preceding example shows, principals were allowed to bring noninstructional problems to the CFC.

Therefore, generally speaking, CFCs were enacted in a manner that diluted the clarity of the learning goal and made the purpose of the CFCs unclear to participants. (See figure 5.1.) Consequently, their effectiveness depended on the particular problem that the presenting principal introduced and how well the principal-facilitator conducted that CFC session. Some CFCs were illuminating and generative; these conversations helped

FIGURE 5.1 *Enactment of CFCs as mapped on the resource use spectrum*

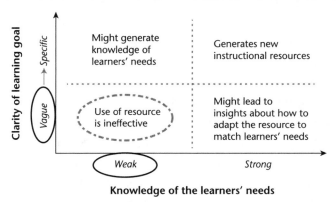

principals see the presented leadership problem differently and often in a more nuanced way. However, the quality of these conversations varied considerably. Arguably, this was because the structure of the conversation did not adhere to the learning purpose. This variability is analogous to the ways in which the use of talking-to-the-text varied among teachers. Without structured support and direct feedback aligned to a clear learning goal, there is no reason to think that the quality of the CFCs would improve or help principals to take smarter instructional leadership actions in their schools.

THE NATURE OF PRINCIPAL LEARNING DURING CRITICAL FRIENDS CONVERSATIONS

Principals' opportunities for learning appeared more purposeful for the group when principals presented problems specifically related to leading instructional improvement. Such problems often were connected to implementing the district's core curriculum, and therefore were common to the group.

To help us further consider how the use of this particular organizational structure both aided and constrained opportunities for principal learning, I offer two examples of Critical Friends Conversations from different principal groups. When the use of the CFC structure adhered to the stated learning purpose and was fitted to the learners' needs, signs emerged that principals' instructional leadership capacity was growing.

Henry's Problem and His Adherence to the CFC Structure

In April near the end of the school year, Henry, a veteran CUSD principal, shared a problem of teaching and learning at his school. This was the first leadership problem explicitly focused on instruction that Henry's group had considered in the first year of CFCs. Henry said, "We've made a lot of literacy improvements at my school, but we're still struggling to determine what proficiency looks like in student work. There are still a lot of inconsistencies in the quality of students' work depending upon the teacher's expectations." As evidence of this variation, Henry brought ten students' reader's notebooks from two different grade levels and two different teachers. Instructional differences between the two teachers were particularly pronounced because the notebooks with the stronger work belonged to the younger students. Henry invited his colleagues to look through the reader's notebooks and see the variation in quality. Henry was also the first principal to bring samples of student and teacher work to a CFC. His colleagues pored over the notebooks. They had lots of questions: Did every grade level use these notebooks? How are the writing tasks connected to the district curriculum? How did Henry get all of the teachers to agree? Questions erupted and pulled the group away from following the CFC protocol.

Returning to the protocol, Henry reiterated his leadership problem and asked his colleagues what they thought he should do to make sure all students were held to a consistent and high standard of learning in his school. Henry's group asked him many "clarifying" questions. As Henry responded, he talked about the important role that the full-time literacy coach at his school had played in driving the teaching and learning progress in his school ("She is a fireball," he said). He explained how the literacy coach had challenged him and pushed him far out of his comfort zone. He described their disagreements and how frustrated the literacy coach got with him, and he with her. He said that many of his teachers didn't like her.

Henry's colleagues focused on his description of the fiery relationship between the literacy coach and the teachers. As Henry answered their questions, it became increasingly clear that he had enormous respect for this coach. He credited her willingness to repeatedly challenge him with helping him to change his own practices and claimed that she did the same for the teachers. Henry's peers did not have a conversation about the specific problem Henry presented. Although Henry did not hear new strategies or different approaches to try out with teachers, the opportunity to talk about an instructional leadership challenge, which he approached so openly and sincerely, led him to voice a deep concern as the CFC protocol concluded: "When our literacy coach leaves the school, I want to have a staff that can sustain the progress we've made, and I want to know how to lead this work." Henry's admission—I want to know how to lead this work—revealed that he recognized his own need to learn how to lead instructional improvement. There was no structure or opportunity, however, for his peers or the district administrators to follow up on Henry's revelation.

Opportunities for Learning Afforded by Henry's CFC

Henry's CFC provided quite a few opportunities for his group to learn. Henry approached the CFC process openly and adhered closely to the protocol. He brought a genuine problem of instructional leadership as well as evidence of his problem for others to see. The reader's notebooks he shared were eye-opening for some principals as they saw the quality of student work that purposeful literacy instruction produced. And how to reduce the variation in instructional quality among teachers was a good model of an instructional leadership problem. Thus the principals in Henry's CFC had multiple opportunities to learn—from Henry's problem, from the stories he shared, and from seeing the reader's notebooks in use at his school.

Although principals were always asked to present their leadership problem along with "one or two key documents," this did not usually happen. As one elementary supervisor who was particularly attentive to how principals followed the CFC routine observed, "Sometimes I've noticed that principals will have the document in front of them, but they won't share it. They've forgotten, and that's a major piece." Through the lens of the instructional capacity building framework, not using the documentation indicates that the purpose of the documents was not clear to the principals and perhaps was also not clear to many of the elementary supervisors.

Robert's Instructional Leadership Problem and His Group's Probing Questions

Another Critical Friends Conversation found a principal struggling to make progress with a "messy" problem: Robert had recently become principal of his school and had inherited a teaching faculty that, while widely trained in a workshop model for literacy instruction, had begun to lose momentum in its implementation of this approach. "I've realized that although I have been supportive of teachers continuing to implement the reading and writing workshop model at [our school], the majority of teachers have continued to move to this work slowly," he said. He pointed to his school's standardized test results, noting that they remained consistently flat, with only half of his (mostly bilingual) student population scoring "proficient" in English language arts. He continued: "I feel like the substitute in a classroom where students have gotten away with doing the minimum throughout the day." He felt challenged in his ability to offer the necessary feedback to teachers to "move their thinking forward" in regard to the workshop model. He struggled to strike a balance between urgency and complacency, and wanted to avoid a leadership approach that came off as "too top-down, too dictatorial."

During the clarifying question portion of the protocol, one colleague wondered if he was collecting any other evidence of teachers' work with the literacy workshop model beyond examining standardized test scores. Robert was not. Moving forward, he might seek new ways to gather such information. Another colleague wondered what other individuals at his school could be designated as "leaders" in helping promote the literacy workshop model. This colleague also noted that he knew there were instructional leaders at Robert's site—and named two coaches. This question invited Robert to consider how his leadership work could be distributed across people in his school.

Writing down probing questions for the next step of the CFC process, principals went deeper into Robert's leadership problem. One question asked him to weigh the positive and negative effects of adopting a "dictator" approach to this problem of teachers not using the reading and writing workshop model. Another suggested he consider what features of the workshop model made him believe so strongly in it. A third colleague simply asked him to reflect more on the ways he conceived of "urgency" when it came to promoting instructional improvement. Indirectly, Robert's colleagues asked him to connect the use of the reading and writing workshop to particular learning goals for students. They suggested that Robert articulate a clear purpose for using this literacy model. None of the principal participants, however, focused on what teachers might need to learn how to do in order to use the reading and writing workshop model more effectively or what currently prevented teachers from using the model. That is, Robert's colleagues considered one dimension of the resource use spectrum but not the other.

Robert decided to respond to the probing question regarding "urgency." He raised the point that, similar to the way principals were being asked to have "courageous conversations" among themselves at these principal meetings, perhaps he, too, could adopt such an approach. By having conversations with teachers that were grounded in honest, constructive feedback and characterized by trust and high expectations, he wondered if he could generate "urgency" among his faculty to use the literacy workshop model.

After thinking aloud about his colleagues' questions, Robert listened to his peers discuss his problem of practice. One colleague offered a suggestion about a specific professional development that trained educators in having such structured "courageous conversations." Another suggested how Robert might benefit from more involvement in grade-level team meetings. A third principal suggested that he fully embrace a dictator approach and simply demand teachers do more with their workshop training. Robert's colleagues made well-intentioned suggestions but none of these were likely to lead to the necessary changes at his school. According to the resource use spectrum, Robert needed a better understanding of what his teachers needed to learn to do as well as a clearer purpose for using the literacy workshop approach at his school in the first place.

When Robert rejoined the conversation, he remarked that it sounded helpful to become more involved in the grade-level teams meetings, as well as to spend more time in classrooms in general. He also began thinking of what other people he might involve in promoting the literacy workshop model. He considered how he could better employ his instructional leadership team in this effort. His colleagues, in turn, shared what they had begun to think about as a result of their participation in this conversation: some pondered the nature of "urgency" and others considered how creating new structures could go hand in hand with the work of instructional improvement.

Opportunities for Learning Afforded by Robert's CFC

As described, the CFC process helped some principals see messy dilemmas more clearly and get ideas from their colleagues about how to think differently about the presented problem. The process helped some principals begin to understand their problem more completely and consider taking new actions to work toward its solution. In Robert's case, the questions his colleagues asked raised questions about his own acts of leadership. Was he collecting evidence of how teachers were implementing the reading and writing workshop model? Was he developing a team to help him lead this instructional change at his school? Were there other conditions—structures or routines—he could create and use at his school? One elementary supervisor said the CFC provided an occasion for a principal to consider a leadership problem: "Listening to their peers gives them some ideas about what to do. That's probably the most powerful . . . I see their faces feeling that they're not alone, other people have had this problem before, and then here's a solution for it. You can see their stress level lightening a little bit."

Because the job of a principal is mostly solitary, the opportunity to talk with peers about difficult problems provided principals with emotional support and camaraderie. Focusing on the challenges of leading instructional change brought principals' collective attention to that aspect of their leadership. The CFCs were an initial step in the direction of building principals' collective capacity to lead instructional improvement.

Through the intimate conversations about a colleague's areas of struggle, principals who previously didn't know each other by name or even by school began to develop professional relationships. As they came to understand each other's struggles, trust grew. As one supervisor explained: "Principals get to hear from their colleagues some of the problems of practice that sometimes they definitely echo. For example, in one of my Critical Friends sessions, there was a principal talking about special education challenges, and immediately they [his colleagues] were like, 'Oh, my gosh, I'm not alone!'"

They also learned which principals had particular expertise (e.g., how to develop a school budget or how to manage a particular special education program) and whom to call on for advice about specific leadership matters. The DES recognized that this was an important outcome of principal meetings: "Somehow they have to learn how to build their relationships [so] they can draw on and bounce off ideas in terms of their instructional challenges." The monthly CFCs enabled the principals to get to know something about each other as leaders. One aspect of becoming a community of practice is developing knowledge about the members because this increases the capacity of the community for social learning. Another condition needed to further group learning is to develop a shared repertoire for how to do the work—here, the work of leading instructional improvement in schools. Developing a shared repertoire for leading instructional improvement was not yet under way among the principals in CUSD.

In addition to providing collegiality and helping principals determine specific actions to take, the CFC process modeled a way principals could think through a problem and work toward formulating a solution. Henry's CFC, which did not adhere to the protocol, showed that the process for thinking through a difficult problem was not well internalized by the principals, even at the end of the first year. Through repeated practice with this conversation routine, however, principals got better at raising questions that pushed the presenting principal to think more deeply about his or her problem.

Here is an example of principals' probing questions after eighteen months of participating in CFCs. The presenting principal told her peer group that she struggled to figure out how to encourage teachers at her school, who had become complacent in their teaching, to challenge students. Her colleagues asked these probing questions: What is the connection you see between increasing rigor and increasing student proficiency? How could you encourage teachers in a safe way to reflect about their level of rigor? What institutional norms are built into your school culture that might inhibit systemic change? Who are your teacher leaders? Have you established relational trust with them? What intentional moves can you make to optimize their [social] capital in your building?

In the second year of using the CFC structure, we saw that principals were more adept at asking probing questions that were "provocative" and that helped the presenting principals better define their expectations and intentions. Participating principals were also better at helping the presenters notice places where their actions didn't match their intentions, which helped principals develop insights about different actions they could take.

Variation in the Groups' Demonstrated Capacity for Learning

Although the groups improved, not all CFC groups increased their capacity to ask probing questions at the same rate. If we consider a group's capacity to ask probing questions as one indicator of the group's capacity for social learning, then we should evaluate which actions the DES took that made it more likely principals would increase their ability to ask probing questions. The decision the DES made to continue using the CFC process for a second year gave principals continued practice with the structure and its routines. The decision in year two to link the CFC and the instructional site visits (ISV)—by having the presenting principal first host the school visit and then present to this same group at the next CFC—also increased the group's understanding of the presenting principal's school environment. As a result, the group was now positioned to ask questions about immediate actions that the host principal had taken following the site visit and to provide encouragement, support, and incentive to take specific actions. (Recall Pat, the teacher at Liberty who claimed that she wanted to use the talking-to-the-text strategy in her teaching but said she needed more social support in her school to be able to do so.)

Missed Learning Opportunities

The DES also missed opportunities to strengthen principals' capacity for learning to lead instructional improvement. For example, DES did not provide principals with direct feedback on how they were participating in the CFCs. Was the leadership problem presented clearly? Was it worthy of group deliberation? Was it a problem of leading instructional improvement? How well was the CFC protocol used and to what effect? DES did not systematically follow up with principals to see if or how they used the knowledge, ideas, strategies, and other resources that emerged during the CFC and ISV processes at school. Evidence is limited about the extent to which CFC practices and the partial solutions that were generated during these conversations actually found their way into the schools. However, without additional support to help CUSD principals actually fit their use of these strategies into their school setting, there is little reason to think that they would have had more success in using the CFC strategies than the teachers at Liberty had in using the Reading Apprenticeship strategies.

Commenting on their participation in the CFC, principals did report things like feeling "challenged to think about my actions as an instructional leader" and "using some of the feedback to assist us in improving our readers and writers workshop implementation schoolwide." However, to increase the likelihood that principals would make significant changes to their instructional leadership—like Molly at Cedar Bridge did in her teaching—it seems reasonable to conclude that principals would need more, and more frequent, opportunities to consider their own leadership actions and evidence of its effects, just as Cedar Bridge teachers had. It is also likely that developing a shared repertoire of instructional leadership practice would have accelerated the individual and collective learning of CUSD principals. Although this was not the case, chapter 7 describes how the DES, through their use of the CFC and ISV structures, began to develop a shared repertoire for leading principal learning. The DES also increased their collective knowledge of what constituted instructional leadership practices by principals.

Robert's Enduring Instructional Leadership Problem

The following year when Robert again took his turn during a CFC session, he presented the same problem of instructional leadership that he had the previous year: "My problem of practice is how readers and writers workshop is or is not being implemented." He said that this year he had "put an instructional leadership team into place," which was a recommendation he received the previous year in his CFC. But, he said, "I can't figure out what to do to help [the teachers]." The members in Robert's CFC group had changed from the previous year. They didn't know that this was the same problem Robert had presented to the group the year before. However, because the DES had linked the CFC structure to the ISV structure in the second year, the principals had visited Robert's school a few weeks prior to the CFC. The principals expected that Robert would have taken some action to begin addressing the problem they discussed at the site visit: that teachers were not sufficiently implementing the new approach to literacy instruction in their classrooms. After listening to Robert's opening statement, one of the principals asked him, "Were you going to tell us anything that you've done since the visit?" The principals waited for Robert's reply. In this moment with this question, Robert's colleagues held him responsible for taking action to improve the quality of teaching and learning at his school. Visibly emotional, Robert said, "I really haven't done much. I shared the information from your visit. I scheduled a mini-lesson PD through the district office." This led his colleagues to ask a series of clarifying questions: "What expectations have you provided to the staff? What resources or supports have you provided? Did you narrow down the aspects of the readers and writers [workshop] approach that you want teachers to choose among and commit to putting into place?" Although Robert appears to have made little progress, the CFC group shows that it has matured in its sense of purpose and in its questioning practices.

MISSED OPPORTUNITIES FOR LEARNING IMPROVEMENT

The discussion of the opportunities for learning that these Critical Friends Conversations afforded also reveal learning opportunities that the DES and the principals did not seize. These missed opportunities are explored in this next section and cast in terms of problems with how the CFCs were used as an instructional resource. Recall from chapter 2 that an instructional resource does not cause learning to occur. Rather, it is how the resource gets used and how well fitted the use is to the learning goals and the learners' needs that engenders learning.

The Follow-Up Problem

The DES frequently commented on the need to "follow up" with principals after CFCs and ISVs. A follow-up mechanism would have functioned as a feedback loop for principals. One district supervisor said, "Once you've shared what your problem of practice is, there needs to be a way to revisit that, not just a one-shot deal." Because the DES's work was so time consuming, they found it almost impossible to conduct such follow-ups with principals in a systematic way. As they reported and we observed, "Leading the work on a daily basis, what it takes to do any one piece of the structures we put in place [requires] hours and hours of time on top of everything else." Following up with principals was just not feasible. One district administrator said,

> I don't think the follow-up necessarily has to be from me. In building the collegiality, maybe a person like the [CFC] facilitator, for example, of that session could be the one to make the phone call: "Hey, just checking in. How's it going with your problem of practice?"

Even when ideas such as this were generated, the DES were rarely able to find the time to share these ideas with their colleagues, let alone put them into practice.

A Lack of Structures and Learning Supports for the DES

In the district supervisors' day-to-day work, they struggled to find time to examine their use of the CFC and ISV structures. There were no analogous learning structures to help them become more effective leaders of principals. Had there been regular structured opportunities for the DES to examine their leadership, they might have had a conversation about the affordances of a more instructionally focused CFC. What supports did the DES need to be able to consider the interdependence of managerial, operational, and instructional leadership problems? Often a principal's presenting problem had components of each. For example, one problem presented at a CFC session was "how to shift grade-level team meetings from a focus on business and logistics to a focus on instruction." Implicit in this leadership problem are issues related to managing people, establishing the structure and operation of grade-level meetings, and communicating expectations for how teachers will use their time. In addition, underlying this problem might be the need to learn how to use grade-level time to focus on instruction rather than the teachers' unwillingness to actually do so. If the DES had had structures and routines to critically examine their own leadership practice, they might have been able to discuss the gap between their espoused purpose for the CFC and their practice. One elementary administrator recognized that the DES's actions did not match their stated intentions when in an interview she said that the DES needed to figure out if the CFCs would "remain just a structure where [principals] have time to talk about what's important to you."

The Problem of Knowing the Learners' Needs

One leadership problem that emerged for the DES, then, was a lack of clarity about what principals most needed to learn from the CFC process. This affected how DES implemented CFCs to support principal learning. For example, even though the protocol provided a sturdy structure to assist principals in having meaningful conversations, not all district administrators expected principals to adhere to the protocol. In one cohort the protocol was loosely used; principals in this cohort did not write down their "probing questions" for each other or read from the facilitator's script. Consultation meetings held with principals in advance to discuss leadership problems provided a way for the DES to learn more about how principals thought about their roles as leaders. However, this knowledge belonged to individual supervisors. Because the DES did not discuss how they structured these conversations to further principals' learning, they were not developing their collective knowledge nor were they developing a shared repertoire of instructional leadership practice among themselves.

The Problem of Aligning the Activity Structure to the Purpose

Providing a narrower and common focus to the CFC problems that principals shared might have done more to develop principals' collective expertise about how to lead instructional improvement. An explicit expectation and support for using what they were learning might have helped the elementary principals construct a shared body of knowledge—including tools, routines, and practices—for leading instructional improvement in their schools. Had the DES been more certain about their own learning goals for principals, then perhaps they could have provided direct feedback to principals about how their selected leadership problem and facilitation of the CFCs served this overarching learning goal. In other words, just as Molly learned to use the talking-to-the-text routine more effectively as she crystallized her learning goal for her students and increased her understanding of their needs, the DES needed to do the same: clarify their learning goals for principals and increase their understanding of what principals most needed to learn in order to lead instructional improvement effectively in their schools.

SUMMARY

The CFC structure marked a striking departure from business-as-usual principal meetings. Principals were grouped together in small cohorts and given structured experiences for talking to each other about aspects of their leadership that they were asked to identify. Principals who previously didn't know one another's names now visited colleagues' schools, looked inside their classrooms, heard what their instructional goals were for students, and discovered how their peers tried to organize teachers' work to achieve these goals. Principals talked with one another and with district administrators about the challenges they confronted in leading these changes in their schools.

From a sociocultural perspective, these are significant changes in how principals spent their time with one another and in how DES interacted with principals to design the principal meetings. These changes, which were sustained over two years, led to positive changes in administrators' relationships with one another and helped supervisors to recognize each other as resources that could support their own instructional leadership. In these ways, the DES helped expand the collective capacity of elementary principals for leading instructional improvement. As the chapter details, the growth was slow. Deep and meaningful change often is. Nevertheless, such changes marked bold organizational steps toward dismantling CUSD's historically top-down decision-making practices by developing routines for two-way communication between district and site administrators and by investing in developing principals' knowledge.

CHAPTER 6

HOW CAN DISTRICTS SUPPORT PRINCIPALS AS INSTRUCTIONAL LEADERS?

Reimagining the Role of the Principal Supervisor

A s the DES sought to strengthen principals' instructional leadership capacity, they realized they also needed to develop this capacity themselves. Developing principals as instructional leaders was new work. Intuitively, the DES perceived that there was a benefit to working together to pursue their mutual goal of improving principals' ability to lead instructional improvement. However, collaborating as a team of administrators for the first time proved to involve learning how to work together, how to lead in a new way, and how to forge their own community of practice to support this new type of work.

RESTRUCTURING THE WORK OF OVERSEEING SCHOOLS

Altering the way that the DES oversaw the daily work of schools presented many challenges. The foremost challenge was the way the central office carried out its work and its conception of the central office's role in relationship to schools. The discussion that follows begins to explain the capacities a central office needs in order to support a different type of leadership to schools.

Learning to Lead in a New Way

As the DES embarked upon this process, they had learning needs of their own. However, these were largely overlooked (or neglected) by their supervisors. Senior district administrators may not have fully recognized the DES's new leadership approach or the training it demanded. And even if they did, senior leaders may not have had the capacity to support the elementary administrators in their new endeavors. Coopersville Unified School District (CUSD) was not unique in its inattention to the learning needs of its district office administrators.

Central offices have traditionally functioned as bureaucracies.[1] In a brief historical account, Richard Elmore claims that "administration in education . . . has come to mean not the management of instruction but the management of the structures and processes around instruction [because] the instructional core is weak and uncertain."[2] A weak instructional core means that the practice of teaching is incapable of being translated into "reproducible behaviors"; thus, Elmore argues, the instructional core is seen as unlikely to be influenced by efforts to evaluate it.[3] Bruce King and Kate Bouchard further describe the bureaucratic role of educational administrators:

> Actions of educational leaders, those charged with steering improvement efforts, have historically mirrored the conventional form of school and district organization. That is, leaders managed a bureaucracy and the workforce within it. . . . Leadership responsibilities were associated with specific, official positions within the hierarchy and tended to focus on administrative matters rather than instructional ones.[4]

The heart of bureaucracy, then, is control and regulation, not learning. Oversight and control are key regulatory functions that serve an important purpose in a system striving for equal opportunity and equitable outcomes. Concerns for more balanced student achievement naturally require some central oversight.[5] However, more recently school reformers and researchers have asserted that central offices also need to become places that engender learning or innovation.[6]

Imagining an Ambidextrous Central Office

To function as an organization that engenders learning requires different practices and competencies from those needed for control and regulation; indeed, these different organizational capacities call for new conceptions of what the core work of the central office is. I argue that both functions are necessary if school districts are to achieve an adequate level of system coherence, assure equitable opportunities for students, and achieve a high standard of learning excellence for all. I propose that district central offices also need to create the conditions for learning. In the language of organizational scholars, central offices need to become ambidextrous organizations. This term offers an instructive concept that is applicable to leadership in the central office. According to organizational theorists, ambidextrous organizations have two distinct capabilities—the capacity to regulate and control as well as to learn and innovate.[7] Scholars point out that these capabilities are fundamentally in tension, but both are critical for organizational survival in the face of environmental change.[8] Thus, scholars conclude that a significant demand is placed upon senior leadership to figure out how to develop the needed dynamic capabilities that can transform their existing organization into an ambidextrous one.

As described by organizational theorists Charles O'Reilly and Michael Tushman, the idea of "*dynamic capabilities* emphasizes the key role of senior leadership to appropriately adapt, integrate and reconfigure organizational skills and resources to match changing environments."[9] In a central office, senior leadership includes the superintendent and his/her cabinet. Instructional capacity building can help central offices know what to do to increase their capacity to learn and innovate. An analogous need exists for central office senior leadership teams to develop the ability to seize opportunities for their own learning—to create new routines and structures within the central office, to reconfigure central office workgroups, and to identify assets located within and outside of the district that are necessary to strengthen the overall quality of learning at each level of the system. The idea is that this ambidexterity will enable central offices to become the hub for district learning while also performing needed regulatory functions.

The argument for central offices to become ambidextrous organizations is rooted in a particular conception of teaching and leading. This view assumes that teaching and leading are inherently nonroutine and complex activities, where challenges are often local, and where problem identification and problem solving is intrinsic to the work of teaching and leading effectively. Thus, to lead schools engaged in such complex and dynamic work—to help them become more effective places of learning—the central office must organize itself to also undertake interdependent and collective work. Its work is embedded in the actions central office administrators take to identify problems and solve them. Invariably, central office solutions will require an array of actions that are context-specific and probably involve some coordinated action and interdependence among people who don't usually work together. These are the dynamic capabilities central offices need; however, they are typically lacking and may not even be recognized by senior leadership as necessary. This was partially the case in CUSD.

Speaking to a group of CUSD principals, a district administrator said:

> When we as individual leaders sit with problems and try to solve them by ourselves, which is often what we think we're getting paid to do, the outcome is uncertain at best. You don't know that you'll get the buy-in, you don't know that you'll account for all the variables, and so in some ways one of the takeaways is, don't let problems just sit with you. You've got to create the structures and the safety so that more and more teachers in schools can be involved in actually naming the right problems and beginning to work on them. And the same is true for us [district administrators]. We shouldn't be trying to name [the problem], we shouldn't be coming up with the structures. That's the way it is done, but it doesn't mean it is effective. . . . We need to involve you

[principals] in naming [the problems] effectively and then thinking through what solutions could look like.

This "epiphany" from a district administrator illustrates both the need for ambidextrous thinking by the central office and its rarity.

The educational research literature acknowledges the absence of such organizational ambidexterity when it reports that districts provide little support to principals on how to lead learning improvement in their schools.[10] A recent study by Meredith Honig and Lydia Rainey (an exception in the research literature because it examines how administrators in one district attempted to help principals learn how to analyze data and develop strategies for accelerating student achievement) also showed that more centralized learning is probably needed for administrators to perform their role effectively.[11] The authors found that the levels of principal engagement and the extent to which principals were asked to partake in challenging instructional leadership activities varied considerably across six principal professional learning communities, which were facilitated by different district administrators.[12] They largely attributed the differences in principals' opportunities to learn to variations in how the learning experiences were facilitated by district administrators. While the important role of the district administrator in enabling or constraining such opportunities is not surprising, it does point to the need for district administrators to receive support in how to facilitate others' learning. Facilitation is a particularly important skill to develop in district administrators who work with principals. In Honig and Rainey's study, they also "found that engaging principals in challenging conversations was fundamental to many of the other practices, especially the use of tools" that seemed to enable principals to learn in these settings.[13]

Both Honig and Rainey's study and my own team's work with CUSD elementary administrators suggest that district administrators who are trying to engage principals in examining their own leadership practices need support to learn how to do so in the most effective manner. Researchers who studied twenty-seven schools in seven districts that were seriously engaged in the work of school improvement had similar findings.[14] At the end of their multiyear study, these researchers concluded:

1. The capacity of the educational system to enhance the practices that produce student learning depends on leadership that focuses on learning improvement for both students and professional staff, and mobilizes effort to that end.
2. The power and sustainability of learning-focused leadership depends, in large measure, on the presence of a multilevel system of leadership support.[15]

The instructional capacity building framework can help us see how to develop such a multilevel system of leadership support.

The DES's ability to learn through their own acts of helping principals develop their capacity to lead instructional improvement was critically important to the overall success of their endeavors. The remainder of this chapter explores the significant and varied challenges that the DES confronted in trying to learn in and from their own leadership practice. Some of the challenges DES faced may have been because their work was separated structurally and conceptually from other district office departments and from the senior leaders in the central office.

LEADING PRINCIPAL LEARNING IS DIFFICULT AND UNFAMILIAR WORK

The DES confronted at least four different types of challenges when they tried to lead principal learning from the central office even as they themselves were learning how to direct this new work, which was continuously evolving. I categorize the challenges that the DES faced as technical, structural, relational, and logistical/organizational challenges. From an instructional capacity building perspective, these challenges are those of insufficient instructional resources. While this chapter describes instructional resources that were missing, chapter 7 details how the DES began to develop its capacity for social learning, for innovation, and for resource creation in order to help principals become more effective instructional leaders.

Technical Challenges

Technical challenges represent the sorts of problems inherent in carrying out this new work. As described in chapter 5, these challenges were abundant. This section describes in greater detail the significant technical hurdles that the DES encountered.

Knowledge Problems The DES did not have strong knowledge about what principals needed to know how to do in order to lead instructional improvement in their schools. Therefore, elementary supervisors ran into problems determining appropriately specific goals for principal learning that would lead to instructional improvement that they could measure and track. The DES also needed to develop knowledge of their own, such as how to develop principals' capacity to achieve the goals that they established. Gaining this knowledge was particularly difficult for a variety of reasons. It required that the DES grasp what leading instructional improvement entailed in sixty school contexts where principals worked as well as understand what individual principals needed to learn how to do. To make effective use of the instructional site visits, the DES also found they needed to know how to facilitate principals' learning when principals felt vulnerable. They needed to know how to help principals draw connections between their classroom observations of students working on tasks and the teaching practices as well as the connections between these tasks and the Common Core Standards. They also needed to help principals to think about what the host principal might do to support teachers' learning based upon their analysis.

When facilitating these sessions, elementary district administrators found that they needed to create conditions that were conducive to group or social learning—a challenging task. The needed conditions—which would lead to asking questions, posing problems, and active listening— were not the same as those needed for information sharing. Many principals had not opened up their schools to one another before, and they felt quite vulnerable. The DES needed to discover how to establish authentic learning conditions for principals as well as for themselves. They also found that they needed to figure out new ways of working with each other that went beyond information sharing. If they were going to develop their own capacity to build principals' instructional leadership skills, then they needed new routines and practices for conducting their work together.

Determining Appropriately Specific Goals for Principal Learning Identifying effective and appropriate goals for principal learning related to leading instructional improvement and establishing expectations for principals was challenging for the DES. The earlier discussions of the CFC described how the DES had difficulty making principals' learning goals specific enough. For goal setting to be effective, three conditions need to be in place: people need to feel personally committed to the goal, they must believe that they have the capacity to achieve it, and the goal needs to be specific enough that people can monitor their progress toward it.[16] As described, the administrators were all personally committed to developing principals' capacity to lead instructional improvement in their schools, and they were reasonably confident that they could achieve this goal. However, they did not have a well-defined or common vision of what leading instructional improvement entailed. Absent this vision, the DES were vulnerable to simultaneously foisting multiple district initiatives onto principals under the guise of school improvement. Initiatives emanated continuously from various departments (e.g., special education, curriculum, assessment, human resources) in the central office. The central office also lacked a coordinated and coherent approach to helping principals improve conditions for student learning in their schools.

The Problematic Learning Goals of Instructional Site Visits The elementary administrators, familiar with the Instructional Rounds process as it was used in other parts of the district, believed that participating in ISVs would be useful to principals. They stated these goals for the ISVs: (1) Principals will participate in school visits using a focused walk-through protocol so that they calibrate on cognitive demand and develop a common understanding of instructional shifts and (2) principals will use this common understanding and apply it to teacher collaboration, assessing student learning, and providing teacher feedback. In an August discussion, the DES further specified the learning purpose of ISVs and articulated three desired learning goals:

1. Help principals know how to improve teachers' instruction. (This goal communicated the DES's desire to make sure principals knew how to analyze student work, including the cognitive demand of student tasks and their alignment to the CCSS.)
2. Hone their equity lens. (This goal was to make sure principals noticed who the struggling students were and what sort of support they needed.)
3. Develop principals' ability to give feedback to teachers and help teachers connect feedback/comments to action (i.e., make instructional changes).

On the surface, these may seem like fine goals. However, closer inspection suggests several problems. The biggest was the relationship between the goals or purpose of the site visits and the activity structure. First, it is not clear how the enacted ISV process, which followed "a consistent protocol for looking at teaching and learning," would help principals know how to give feedback to teachers or what to do to help teachers improve their instruction. Second, the criteria about what counted as improvement on these three goals was absent, and so measuring progress was difficult.

Using ISVs to Develop Principals' Capacity to Achieve Established Learning Goals Viewed through the lens of the instructional capacity building framework, we can examine the decision to adopt the ISV structure in the same way we might analyze the decision to adopt any other sort of instructional resource. As we saw in chapter 3, teachers were not equally effective in their use of the talking-to-the-text instructional approach. The spectrum of resource use provides a way to understand how likely it is that a particular resource will be used effectively. Using this tool, we can conclude that for the ISVs to help achieve the stated principal learning goals, the DES would need to (a) have a clear learning purpose in mind for employing the ISV structure, (b) understand the features of ISVs well enough to know what learning opportunities this structure could provide, and (c) have sufficient knowledge of the principals' learning needs related to their learning goals. In other words, the DES needed to know what principals already knew how to do with regard to improving teachers' instruction, employing an "equity lens," and providing teachers with meaningful feedback on their teaching.

However, this was not knowledge that the DES had historically gathered in a systematic way. Furthermore, changes among the DES and changes to school assignments as well as the steady turnover of school principals made knowing the learning needs of individual principals difficult. For the DES to use ISVs to deepen principals' knowledge of how to improve teachers' instruction, they also needed to understand how the ISV routine would enable principals to learn about instructional practice—including the qualities that make instruction effective—as well as how to give teachers feedback and other ways to help teachers shift their instruction.

The Content of the ISVs Varied   Viewing instances of classroom instruction had the potential to provide rich content for a conversation about instruction: what students were asked to do, how engaged they were in the learning activity, and whether the observed teaching-learning episode adhered to the Common Core Standards or provided evidence of "instructional shifts." This was the imagined "content" for the principals' conversation. The quality of the analysis that principals did following the observations, however, was influenced by the instruction they observed, by the quality of their observations, and by the facilitator's ability to structure a conversation about the content. The extent to which principals developed knowledge of instructional quality, equitable instruction, and giving teachers meaningful feedback, then, turned on the quality of the teaching witnessed in the classrooms and the quality of the discussion afterward. That discussion relied heavily on principals' observations of student and teacher actions, which were reconstructed from principals' notes and perspectives on the observed lesson.

The nature and quality of principals' observations depended, of course, upon the individual observers—their values and knowledge of teaching and learning, which varied significantly from principal to principal. This meant that the DES's goals for these ISV conversations needed to be clear and the DES needed to provide a structured approach for analyzing the classroom observations. Even with clear goals and a structure for analysis, ensuring that these discussions resulted in the desired learning was difficult for administrators to control because principals observed in *different classrooms*. And even when they observed in the same classroom and focused specifically on student actions, principals noticed and "scripted" *different aspects of learning.*

Principals were told to write down "what students are hearing, reading, saying, and writing" and pay attention to the amount of "teacher talk versus student talk." Making student actions the focus of the observations was intended to focus principals' attention on students' opportunities for learning. However, to see what led to those opportunities, principals also needed to pay attention to the teaching-learning relationship and recognize that interrelationship. Another goal for principal learning, giving feedback to teachers, resided in seeing how principals communicated and worked with teachers. This principal practice was not observed during the ISVs.

The ISV Structure Varied Among Administrator Facilitators Because the district elementary supervisors did not participate in an ISV together, they each had developed somewhat different ideas of how to structure these visits and how to facilitate the discussions that followed the classroom observations. As might be expected, the DES ran into various technical challenges as they implemented the ISV structure. They found that designing learning experiences to meet the varied needs of principals—including those who were new to the principal role, those who had many years of experience, and those who were new to their schools—was difficult. They also found it challenging to facilitate the classroom debriefs during the ISVs. As one principal supervisor put it: "You're leading this group to learning. On a school visit, you are understanding where principals are, where they need to get to understand the standards deeper. You need to know where they need to go next in terms of understanding what students are actually doing. There's so much learning taking place."

This supervisor described many types of learning that the facilitator was engaged in when leading the classroom observation discussions.

Some of this in-the-midst-of-action learning was necessary because the facilitators did not always work closely with the particular principals in their ISV group. Thus, facilitators were trying to figure out what principal participants needed to learn—and they noticed that principals' learning needs were quite varied. Facilitation was made even more challenging because the facilitator often needed to determine in the moment which learning objective to focus on. In other words, which of the three ISV learning goals (if any of these) were relevant in that moment to the observations that the principals were making about the observed classroom.

Structural Challenges

Structural challenges refer to the organizational structures within CUSD, particularly within the central office, that did not readily support the work that the DES were trying to do.

Central Office Was Not a Conducive Environment for Administrator Learning   In CUSD the central office occupied several floors of a large office building where various district departments were housed, including facilities and operations, human resources, the legal department, professional learning, research and assessment, curriculum and instruction, and school supervision. The DES formed a subgroup of the school supervision department. Several central office spaces housed these departments. Each was associated with leading, directing, overseeing, and supporting different aspects of the district's approximately 150 schools, and each department had its own organizational structure and designated resources.

Organizationally as well as conceptually, the central office carried out its work in relatively autonomous ways. In practice, members of these departments—and sometimes subgroups within a department—viewed their work as largely self-contained and isolated from the work that went on in other district departments, even though multiple departments shared the mutual goal of improving student learning outcomes in Coopersville's schools. This meant that members of the curriculum and instruction department did not necessarily work closely with members of the school supervision department to plan and coordinate instructional supports to schools. Within departments, work units did not necessarily coordinate among themselves either. For example, within the school supervision department, elementary supervisors did not coordinate their work with middle school or high school supervisors.

The School Supervisory Department Was a Disjointed Group   There were many administrators with school supervisory responsibilities in CUSD. Approximately a dozen administrators supervised principals within the district. Although these administrators constituted a single department within the central office, they operated in isolated subgroups according to the school level (elementary, middle, or high school) that they supervised. Not surprisingly, they approached their work independently. So when the DES reimagined their work and relationship vis-à-vis principals, their actions did not represent a shared conception or approach to leadership within the school supervision department.

There had recently been a lot of turnover among the elementary supervisors. Six of the seven had been hired in the past two years and were new to their supervisory role. One member was new to the district. Three members were formerly principals in CUSD. It is worth noting that the members of this group had different titles, levels of responsibility, and positional authority within the district: three were responsible for overseeing twenty schools apiece; the other four members reported to them. The higher-ranking members of the group reported directly to the deputy superintendent. One member did not have any principal supervisory responsibilities, which afforded her a somewhat different relationship to the principals and in subtle ways set her apart from the rest, who did supervise principals. In addition to these group membership dynamics, there was no formally appointed group leader. Oversight of the group by the deputy superintendent was minimal. Thus, the group was able to form its own norms, routines, and decision-making processes. Operating as an autonomous group enabled some intragroup social learning. However, the absence of district goals to guide and anchor their work also limited the DES's ability to contribute to the growth of the district's overall instructional leadership capacity.

The Structure of Supervisory Responsibilities Promoted Isolation and Competition The central office culture and the supervisory responsibilities of the DES did not readily promote a shared approach to their leadership work. The responsibilities for school oversight were subdivided among pairs of elementary supervisors, with each pair responsible for one-third of the schools. This longstanding division of labor among the school supervisors had historically led elementary supervisors to operate independently; at times they were even in competition with one another. One member of DES pointed out the change that had occurred in elementary supervisors' working relationships: "There's seven leaders who have never worked with each other before, and now we're working together."

In practice, the divided supervision meant that the DES were not collectively responsible for the performance of the sixty schools. Furthermore, in the eyes of the district, the job performance of the elementary supervisors was based upon the achievement gains of their assigned schools. In addition, because assigning schools to district supervisors was a prominent organizing structure in CUSD, resource allocations were frequently made to schools through their supervisor. This meant that the district elementary supervisors were sometimes in the position of advocating for scarce resources on behalf of their particular schools. For instance, one supervisor described the resource advocacy role this way: "[Sometimes] I need to pick up a phone and say, 'Hey, you know that thing that you were presenting? My schools really need to have access to that,' or . . . if there's a grant, [I may need to make] sure that my schools are included in that grant." The result was that elementary supervisors tended to view their work primarily in terms of their assigned schools, not all those in the district. Some were more inclined to think this way than others. For example, one supervisor described his year's goals in terms of helping his assigned schools succeed: "I would like to ensure that *all of my sites* are healthy and on the road to implementing the Common Core . . . [and able] to actually reflect on their practices so that they can get better at what they do."

Another supervisor also described her goals in terms of the specific schools she was responsible for, but in more personal terms:

What I'd like to have accomplished is building on those relationships with the principals, having the schools and student learning move towards improvement. That's the most important. We have to remember that what we're doing is for the students and for the kids, and even though we're not as directly involved in that work, that's what it boils down to. Supporting the principals. I'd like the principals to feel like I had supported their work and encouraged them and inspired them to do some greater things for their school.

The district elementary supervisors worked hard to develop relationships with their "assigned" principals. This relational work, however, was made difficult because the central office kept reshuffling their assignments. With an annual reassignment of principals to supervisors for three years in a row, it became almost impossible for them to sustain and deepen a working relationship from one year to the next. This repeated reassignment of supervisors to schools appeared to hamper improvement progress within the schools.

The Principal Supervisor Role Gets Reimagined While some elementary administrators were more inclined to view their supervisory role in terms of their relationship to their assigned subgroup of principals, a few indicated a sense of responsibility for all sixty principals. For example, one elementary supervisor said,

By the end of the school year I would like to have . . . change[d] the culture of professional learning, . . . all the shifts that we've put in place, so that principals feel like they're now in professional learning networks themselves, that every principal within the sixty schools feels that direct link to student learning.

Another elementary supervisor said,

What I was really hoping—moving from last year into this year—was . . . for things to be a little bit more concrete around some structures that were aligned across all three [supervisors'] groups of schools.

> I'm hoping . . . people will have gotten into a habit or a pattern of ex-
> pecting that we do a school visit once a month . . . that we're [asking]
> deeper questions and having deeper conversations and that we're even
> shifting the language of the conversations—that we're asking about
> standards. We're asking, "How do you know? What is your evidence?"
> And we're really trying to have [principals] be more critical. . . . I'm
> hoping that we're going to start to see that shift, and that leading into
> next year, we're going to continue on with these same practices.

And finally, a third elementary supervisor expressed his individual goals in terms of not only what he wanted all principals to learn, but also what he hoped the DES would learn:

> For me, my year focus has been on helping myself and helping the
> team [DES] understand the impact of all of the investments that we
> make, money and time. We have an impressive plan. Every time I hear
> one of us describe it to somebody else, I realize how much we've taken
> on. But we don't have a good way yet to measure the impact of all that
> time and money on teacher practice.

Notice that this administrator's comment focuses on teaching as the ulti-mate indicator of the DES's work. Yet the DES did not engage in any direct work with teachers; they worked directly with principals. The administra-tor's focus is understandable, especially given the overriding emphasis in the district to show improvement on student learning outcomes. Teach-ers are most able to influence student learning. In the language of mea-surement, changes to teachers' instructional practice are better viewed as lagging indicators of the DES's efforts, rather than leading indicators. The DES also needed a way to measure and see how principals' practices changed. To this administrator's point, there were no mechanisms in place to observe the effects of the DES's new leadership on principals' practices, or how the DES's work with principals was in turn affecting their work with teachers.

Given the realities of the role of an elementary supervisor in CUSD, it is a testament to this group's commitment to improve the learning opportunities for principals that they wanted to band together and develop a shared approach to support principals. As chapter 5 describes, a confluence of factors within CUSD led the DES to envision a new purpose for the principal meetings and then design different structures, routines, and practices to achieve that purpose.

Isolated Departments Within the Central Office The supervisory department was one of many departments within CUSD. As noted above, each of the central office departments operated relatively independently. The separation and compartmentalizing of their work, whose ultimate aim was to improve instruction and learning environments in the schools, created a level of operational incoherence. An elementary supervisor described one example:

> I see a lot of disconnect between the curriculum and instruction office and the supports and the conversations and the collaborations that need to be had [and] that aren't being had. Prime example: the English language learners (ELL) department that now has the English language development new standards needs to be talking to the curriculum people, and those conversations aren't being had.

Teachers, principals, and district administrators all experienced this incoherence at various times.

With regard to supporting schools' adoption of the district core curriculum, another supervisor was critical of the central office for not pooling the resources across different departments and working in a more coherent way to support individual schools: "We have to use more resources and be more strategic. . . . It's kind of hard to do it alone as [the elementary supervisors]. . . I was hoping this would come from Curriculum and Instruction, but I think for whatever reason, there's a lack of that kind of collaboration or communication to jointly do the work."

A compounding problem was that each department in the central office worked directly with individual school sites. In practice, this meant that a principal might receive requests from multiple central office departments simultaneously. A third supervisor remarked that this created confusion for some principals who "don't know what is [and isn't] a priority. . . everything that comes at them is a priority." This administrator, who had also worked outside of CUSD, thought principals could be better supported by a team of people within the central office who operated as a central clearinghouse of information, especially if this team represented different expertise to help principals manage various problems such as student attendance, special education needs, and student behavioral issues. The decentralized supports and the isolated manner in which district departments operated meant that frequently a principal would have to navigate multiple departments within the central office bureaucracy to resolve a problem at the school site. This is what one of the district supervisors referred to as "a lot of other red tape or hurdles that [principals] have to jump." This supervisor thought providing additional central office personnel to help principals "is nice because a principal can then call someone to get access to that department," but warned that "it doesn't necessarily mean that [the help is] structured in a way that will best support that school site, or the teacher, or the principal."

Tensions Within and Between Central Office Departments   Related to the decentralized infrastructure, central office departments had become accustomed to disseminating information to principals during principal meetings by making announcements or handing out printed information. This is part of a district's capacity to regulate and control. Consequently, when the DES changed the structure and content of its principal meetings, they had to educate other departments within the central office about the changed purpose and structure of these meetings. For some departments, this change was an inconvenience as it disrupted their communication routines or presented other problems associated with the loss of easy access to the principals. CUSD had not yet developed an ambidextrous mindset. Some researchers who have studied what happens in schools when the use of resources gets changed have noticed that "using school resources more effectively takes courage because it means setting priorities and being strong enough to say that some things are simply more important than others—even when these priorities demand ending a cherished program."[17] This observation also holds true for the DES's decision to use principals' meeting time differently. The changed purpose of these meetings created some tensions, particularly among administrators in different departments who wanted an audience with sixty principals.

Some of the DES didn't like the strained relationships that emerged with other district administrators: "I don't like the fact that when people want to come and talk to the [principal] group, it's almost like they need an act of Congress to speak to the principals when I know that they need that information." This supervisor recounted a situation in which members of the human resource department wanted to address the principals about new hiring procedures. He felt "frustrated because I think what they have to say is important and principals do need to know it. . . . But I can't say, 'Yes, come.' I have to come back to this body [DES]." Elementary supervisors experienced a loss in their ability to make decisions autonomously. Other supervisors felt they were protecting principals' time by limiting these sorts of announcements in the meetings.

Understandably, the seven-member team sometimes found themselves at odds with their administrative colleagues in the central office, or even disagreeing with each other. When the group first embarked upon its joint work, these tensions were particularly pronounced.

Relational Challenges

The DES faced some challenges, especially at the outset, in terms of their relationships with one another as they learned how to work together. One supervisor's experience was typical: "There are things I want to do, but I feel somewhat constrained because the other two groups [don't], and then I'll hear that they are being entrepreneurial and doing other things." This supervisor described wanting to be a team player but feeling "caught in the middle . . . somewhat restricted" in terms of the decisions he thought he should make to be a good team member versus what he wanted to do for his group of principals.

Lack of Communication Lack of communication and transparency among the DES also emerged as problems in the early months. For example, two were frustrated that they were hearing about professional development work that was happening between administrators and principals in a large district meeting rather than in the more intimate setting of their weekly DES meetings: "[My DES colleague] never mentioned that . . . he's never shared that he's done that. . . . Why do we have to hear about [his] work in a separate meeting? Why aren't we sharing that type of stuff here [in DES meetings]?" By midyear, it was clear that some unspoken tensions were festering within DES. These seemed to stem from uncertainty among individual members as to whether their first allegiance should be to their principals or to their administrator colleagues.

Different Conceptions of What Leading Instructional Improvement Entails
Differences of opinion began to emerge among the DES about what they needed to do to help principals become better able to lead instructional improvement in their schools. One supervisor thought that leading instructional improvement was in large part a matter of "allocating resources" such as the use of time and money, and being able to connect data analysis to the "systems and routines" in the school. Another supervisor said,

> Site administration is a balancing act. The management skill is equally as important as the instructional leadership skill. It's a combination of all that you can gel together to make a successful administrator. In terms of helping a principal grow in the area of instructional leadership, you have to know what they know and what they don't know, and then slowly provide them with information.

This supervisor described principals who needed support in managing their school so that they could have time to focus on improving instruction. He thought a key principal practice for leading instructional improvement was visiting teachers' classrooms because, in his view, this was the basis upon which to provide teachers with feedback: "If the principal doesn't know how to manage time, for example, there's no way they know how to get into the classroom."

A third supervisor saw a great need for developing principals' knowledge of instruction:

I feel like some of the structures we have in place are . . . to increase the knowledge base for our principals about what we mean by good teaching, balanced literacy, implementing the new math units and those math tasks that we're asking principals to do, because this is not only new learning for the teachers, it's new learning for the principals.

Finally, a fourth supervisor described a broader goal for principals: "At the end of the day, I hope that principals can manage a learning system that has the Common Core standards at its center . . . always trying to pull people back to the set of aspirations represented in the standards, comparing actual product to envisioned product."

Their differences affected their work in important ways. For instance, these views influenced whether or not the DES guided principals to bring instructional leadership problems to their Critical Friends Conversations. That their views differed is not surprising since they had not spent time talking about the specific practices of principals who were able to effectively lead instructional improvement, nor had the district provided a vision of what principals who lead instructional improvement effectively actually do.

Logistical and Organizational Challenges

Several logistical challenges arose for the DES as they introduced new structures to principal meetings in order to focus principals' attention on learning to lead instructional improvement.

The Scale of the Work Working with sixty schools is a challenging task. The ratio of one administrator to ten schools in CUSD was much smaller than in other districts, where supervisors worked with as many as thirty schools.[18] Nevertheless, working with ten schools presented logistical challenges to some of the structures that the DES designed. This was particularly true for the monthly instructional site visits. As one supervisor commented, "Now we have, like, fifteen groups running." By design, ISVs occurred three mornings each month, when three pairs of elementary supervisors accompanied small groups of approximately seven principals each on a site visit. Elementary supervisors conducted their ISVs on the same days at the same time. This may have eased the logistical burdens of coordinating the movements of so many individuals, but it meant they were not able to observe each other facilitating these visits. As one supervisor remarked, "Now that we've grown it to sixty schools and four facilitators, we just haven't come back at all and calibrated to see are we doing it the same—we don't see each other."

The Isolated Nature of Their Work   An unanticipated consequence of working out of sight from one another—much the way teaching occurs in isolation from other teachers—was that the DES did not know if principals in different groups were having similar learning experiences. Nor did they have a way to examine and collectively consider the leadership practices that they were developing. As the DES realized that they didn't know how they were all approaching these conversations, their desire to find out and learn from one another grew. They started to talk about the need "to calibrate" their facilitation, which meant "making sure that we're all on the same page moving forward, because it's very, very hard being at a site when you have different expectations."

Difficulty Tracing the Connection from Principals' Learning Opportunities to Action   Another logistical challenge that the DES confronted was figuring out how to follow up with principals to see if they acted upon the suggestions made to them during ISVs or CFCs. One principal supervisor said,

> I would like to follow up better. That would probably be my biggest move. . . . We do the follow-up now where people say what they did, but I'm not calling people; . . . I'm not visiting and saying: *What's happened? Where is your evidence of it?* . . . So much of my time is built into actually doing [ISVs and CFCs] and prepping for [them] and everything else.

The large number of schools that the DES was trying to support, in addition to the other responsibilities of their job, including the planning that each ISV and CFC required, exacerbated the difficulty of following up. Another supervisor described the problem this way:

> You set up the structures, but it's the maintenance of the learning networks. . . . You create it, but then it's ongoing—the amount of time that myself and my team members spend on every single activity that we do on top of everything else—each school visit takes hours to organize, and then you facilitate and you debrief. So, if we just took that one piece of [leading principal learning through] a school visit, it's hours and hours of time.

When the elementary administrators designed these structures, which were quite a bit more time-consuming to prepare for than the previous principal meetings, their other job responsibilities were not reduced. Other administrators also described "a heavy managerial aspect that you need to maintain and do" as part of the job. Again, this problem of the new work conveys that designing, leading, and facilitating principal learning was unfamiliar work in the central office, and supervisor roles were not well designed for carrying out this work. Consequently, supervisors described trying to maintain a focus on instructional leadership as

> an extreme tension or challenge when you're also supervising schools at that managerial level. Every day, when you walk in, you're constantly being pulled as a leader (similar to a principal) in other directions. . . . [To make sure] your time is focused on instruction . . . means everyone's really working two or three jobs at once, because those other [managerial] pieces are so crucial and take a lot of time.

Even though the DES could not figure out logistically how to learn what effect these experiences were having on principals' leadership, they felt strongly that the intention of these experiences was to stimulate principals to take purposeful action in their schools.

One supervisor expressed concern that principals might not be making any changes to their leadership practice: "I feel that with the way of facilitating those visits, it [is] meaningless unless there [is] some follow-through. It cannot be a one-time thing." Another colleague agreed that "a follow-up would always help" but volunteered, "I don't think the follow-up necessarily has to be from me. . . . I don't think . . . that I need to be in charge and micromanage. . . . Some people do a little too much; . . . sometimes you just need to let people be. You guide them the best way that you can, . . . but you don't need to always be watching everything that happens." Nevertheless, the DES agreed that they wanted more information about how, if at all, principals were changing their approach to leading their schools.

NO TIME FOR PAYING ATTENTION TO THE DES'S OWN LEARNING

Given the demanding nature of the job of supervisor, as well as the newness of these various structures, the DES had difficulty paying attention to their own learning needs. Early on, they began asking, "How are we going to get better?" At a September meeting, one supervisor wondered, "How do we know that what we are doing is making an impact?" Another asked, "How is the principals' level of thinking changing? How are we measuring impact on the classroom?" A third said, "We want to create a community that allows us to know that a school is really moving."

From the outset of their undertaking, the DES recognized that "we will probably need to use our own time differently," and they talked about various documented aspects of school practice that they might want to examine: "faculty meeting notes, professional development plans, tough special education cases, and how to respond to a whole constellation of issues that come up." They also had the idea of conducting their own Critical Friends Conversations as a way to put their own leadership challenges in front of each other and examine their own leadership practice. One supervisor said, "I'd like to do a Critical Friends." Another noted, "Once a month doesn't feel like enough—maybe we present every other week." A third said, "I'd like us to work on the absurd and hypocritical policies that we have to jump through . . . and the fourteen things that people need to sign off on." A fourth supervisor commented, "I've had issues with a particular elementary school and this might be my Critical Friends: How do you decide which principal you are going to go see when you wake up in the morning?" In spite of their initial enthusiasm and interest in using some of their weekly meeting time to participate in their own Critical Friends process or to examine documents that show examples of principal instructional leadership, they were not able to organize themselves to actually do so as a regular part of their weekly meetings.

Initially, the DES did not make regular time to examine the effects of their new leadership structures and practices on principals' performance. Although they met every week for three hours, in the early months they did not typically set aside any of this time to talk about their own leadership practices. They agreed that "there's a reflection piece that we don't get to do as a district. We don't have a time to reflect." No one else in the district was paying attention to their learning needs; they were not being encouraged to take time to examine the effects of their work. Furthermore, they each had enormous demands placed upon their time by their vast job responsibilities.

When the principal supervisors had their first interviews with us as part of our study, some commented on the opportunity that the interview gave them to reflect on their practice. One supervisor said, "This [time to think about my work] doesn't happen. There's nowhere where that happens. . . . There's this learning network that we've now provided for principals, but [we need to] make sure that we have some time to do that for ourselves." They recognized that they needed to set aside time to take stock of their work and that trying to do so in the midst of their daily schedules was too challenging. So, the DES planned a full-day retreat midyear to consider the effects of their own instructional leadership.

A Retreat Designed to Spur Learning and Improve Leadership The DES asked for outside help to facilitate this day. At the retreat, they spent time looking closely at their own practice. All agreed this was an important opportunity for learning, for strengthening their identity as a team, and for making a commitment to each other and to continued learning. The DES found this time so valuable that they planned a second retreat for June at the end of that first year. Making time to reflect on the effects of their work in schools still seemed impossible for them to manage as part of their weekly schedule. At the end of their first retreat in January, they wondered aloud:

- "How do we maintain this level of discussion to wrestle through ideas about being effective to support principal learning?"
- "How do we keep going deeper, keep putting evidence of our impact on the table, keep comparing this evidence to what we want, and keep refining our practices?"
- "How to have more time in our weekly meetings for deep reflection tied to evidence?"

The logistical and organizational challenges inherent in their work, as well as the enormous and varied responsibilities they had, seemed inescapable. It's what led one administrator who did not have school supervisory responsibilities to observe: "My colleagues spend so much of their time worrying about a gas leak at a school, or this and that." The constant operational and managerial demands of the job pulled leaders' attention at each level of the system away from maintaining their focus on the most important matters of teaching and learning.

SUMMARY

The discussion of the many and various types of challenges that the DES confronted when they began to fundamentally alter the way they conceived of and conducted their work with principals reveals the magnitude of changes needed within the district system for it to significantly improve. This chapter has argued that the central office needed to develop its capacity to become an ambidextrous organization in order to adequately support the supervisors in their work. The instructional capacity building framework suggests various resources that the central office needed to recognize and/or develop to grow its ambidextrous capacity, such as organizational structures that conceptually and practically support joint work within and across central office departments and knowledge of the skills and practices that district administrators need to possess in order to provide effective leadership.

The vast and multilevel interdependencies within the district system began to emerge in this chapter. They show the complexity of the system at each level. Given these system-level challenges and inherent complexity involved in DES's work to improve opportunities for principal learning, it was clear to the supervisors and to us as outside researchers that they needed more support for their own learning. Chapter 7 describes several ways the DES developed their capacity to learn.

CHAPTER 7

HOW CAN DISTRICT LEADERS LEARN TOGETHER?

A Research-Practice Partnership

In this chapter I describe several important ways that our researcher-practitioner relationship helped the DES develop its capacity for social learning. I also illuminate a potential role researchers can play to help central office leadership teams build their capacity for leading instructional improvement.

The central office in a school district needs to engender learning and innovation in addition to exercising oversight and control. As discussed in chapter 6, to have both capacities is to be an ambidextrous organization. Opportunities for central office leaders to learn are rare—but also critical for developing the capabilities needed to become an ambidextrous organization. I describe how researchers can help central offices achieve this goal.

DEVELOPING THE CAPACITY TO LEARN AND INNOVATE

To develop these dynamic capabilities, central office work teams need to (a) seize opportunities for their own learning, (b) create new routines and structures for learning, (c) reconfigure their work groups, and (d) identify assets located in and outside of the district that can help strengthen the overall quality of teaching and learning. Developing these capabilities is one way that a district team, such as the DES, can expand its capacity to lead principals in their efforts to improve teaching and learning.

Unable to routinely reflect upon their work—a problem discussed in the preceding chapter—the DES organized full-day retreats to consider the impact of their work. From an instructional capacity building perspective, the retreats represented an organizational structure that the DES instituted to support their learning. The DES called upon my research team to facilitate its retreats, which occurred three times during our two-year study. We, in turn, developed tools, materials, and practices to aid the DES's learning. These instructional leadership resources are described in this chapter.

The DES's Joint Work

To develop the dynamic capabilities associated with learning and innovating, the elementary supervisors needed to conceive of their work as collective work. When the DES created and began using common structures for principal learning, such as the Critical Friends Conversations (CFCs) and the instructional site visits (ISVs), they began to think of their leadership as joint work. Using these common structures, as one supervisor said, opened up the possibility for them to look at "the quality of the interactions inside of those structures." With common structures and practices (e.g., principal-supervisor conversations to select problems of leadership practice), it became possible for the DES to examine how they approached leading instructional improvement as individuals. In so doing, they could begin to develop a shared repertoire of instructional leadership practice. However, because the elementary supervisors were busy engaging in the work, they needed someone to plan and facilitate this learning.

Moreover, the supervisors' interest in and commitment to work together did not mean they knew how to do so. In sociocultural terms, the DES needed to learn how to become a community of practice and to develop their capacity for social learning. Much has been written about communities of practice since Etienne Wenger wrote his book on the topic in 1998. As discussed in chapter 1, in his research Wenger described the social process of learning whereby individuals learn through participation and by pursuing specific competencies to be able to do something in particular.[1]

For example, Wenger and Jean Lave have also written about examples of communities of practice, such as Alcoholics Anonymous and quilting circles.[2] By their definition, a community of practice exists when a group of individuals come together regularly for a particular purpose. In such a group, *the practice* is the source of coherence of the community.[3] This means that the actual practices that members in the community enact, and the extent to which these practices are common practices connected to a shared goal, determines the degree of coherence within a community.

For instance, the principals who participated in monthly CFCs resembled a community of practice, but the CFCs were missing some key features. As the CFC analysis in chapter 5 suggests, it did not appear that principals were pursuing specific competencies or common practices through their participation in the CFC. And, in the first year of the project, the way CFCs were enacted showed that many CFCs did not really focus on supporting principals to do something in particular—to lead instructional improvement in their schools. Thus, communities of practice might be viewed as forming within the CFC structure. The more the practices comprised in the CFC were tightly connected to developing principals' *instructional* leadership capabilities, the greater the coherence and learning capacity of the CFC became. Thus, strong communities of practice connected to the goal of improving teaching and learning are a mechanism for growing instructional capacity.

Becoming a Community of Practice

In effect, the district elementary supervisors were in the early stages of becoming a community of practice. They shared a purpose for working together: to develop principals as instructional leaders. These administrators were also committed to their own learning. One supervisor described this interest in learning: "I'm hoping to become an even better instructional leader, learning things I don't know, learning strategies and protocols and ways of thinking around our work. I think [the research partnership] can help with that." Over two years, we observed ways in which the DES developed their ability to support principals in becoming leaders of instructional improvement in their schools. Through our partnership, we believe we contributed to the DES's growing capacity.

One way to understand if and how the DES were developing their capabilities to learn and to lead instructional improvement is to pay attention to the DES's actions, including the ways in which their capacity for social learning evolved over time. What was the evidence that the DES were becoming their own community of practice? Wenger theorized three aspects of the relationship between "practice" and "community" that matter for furthering learning within a community: there must be mutual engagement of participants, the work needs to be viewed as a joint enterprise, and practitioners need to develop a shared repertoire for doing things.[4] The remainder of this chapter examines the role that the research team played in helping the DES develop a "shared repertoire" for developing principals' capacity to lead instructional improvement and the extent to which the DES viewed this work as a joint enterprise.

OUTSIDERS: THE ROLE OF THE RESEARCHER

Researchers conducting fieldwork are uniquely situated to be both observers and learners. It is the researcher's job to look closely, to take in the specific while also noticing the larger context in which events are situated. A researcher who is a keen observer will pay attention to the nuances of the environment, will notice people's emotions, will attend to the particular circumstances of a situation, and will seek to discover the variations and patterns in the lived experiences they observe and participate in. When researchers have systematic and structured opportunities to share what they are noticing with participants, new opportunities for learning are created.

Conducting fieldwork, as Harry Wolcott describes it, is about "learn[ing] something of the way some other group of people lives and thinks."[5] To accomplish this necessarily requires some sort of "involvement" with others. As Wolcott explains, "Fieldwork knowledge entails intimate personal knowledge of the contextualized lives of others."[6] Acquiring such knowledge requires spending a great deal of time in a place and keenly observing what happens there. The fieldwork that I conducted in Coopersville Unified School District occurred over a six-year period in which I spent many hours observing and working with teachers, principals, and district administrators. During some of this time, I also had the help of research assistants. Over time and because of the various ways that I was involved with people in CUSD, I came to know some of them and how they approached their work as leaders, teachers, and learners. As Wolcott puts it: "[B]ecoming a *genuine participant* in at least some activities of a group over a period of time, or acting in slightly more reserved capacities such as *observing participant* or *privileged observer*, are far different ways of gathering far different data from the sort of 'neat' data most researchers seek and get."[7]

Some of the data that I "got" and the approaches I used for "getting" this data are briefly described in this chapter as a way to explain how the researcher role was used to help create some of the conditions that enabled the DES to learn in and from their instructional leadership work. Of course, as an observing participant, these were occasions for my learning too.

A Learning Partnership

As described in part 1 of this book, relationships oriented toward learning are an important aspect of building instructional capacity. Relationships based upon learning are also relatively rare. This may be because learning relationships require an investment of time, care, and trust as well as a shared commitment to learn something in particular. Researchers who are committed to simultaneously studying and helping to solve enduring educational problems of practice sometimes engage in a type of educational research known as design-based implementation research (DBIR).[8] Studies that adhere to the tenets of DBIR have four key elements: (1) a focus on persistent problems of practice; (2) a commitment to iterative, collaborative design; (3) a concern with developing theory related to both classroom learning and implementation through systematic inquiry; and (4) a concern with developing capacity for sustaining change in systems.[9] This approach to conducting research positions the researcher and the practitioner in a mutually rewarding relationship where each other's knowledge and perspective is sought out and valued as part of a joint enterprise to learn something in particular. In our work with the DES, we followed a DBIR approach. We did so because we wanted to understand what was required for district administrators to learn how to lead principals to become instructional leaders and how to develop the conditions for learning in the central office. We also believed that a researcher-practitioner partnership could assist the DES in their desire to learn in and from their instructional leadership and simultaneously help them increase their instructional leadership capacity.

In addition to adhering to these four tenets of DBIR, our research practice partnership was predicated upon the notion that in order to develop capacity for changing the system effectively, as well as sustaining change in the system, our district partners would need opportunities to learn through the work that they were embarking upon—and so would we as researchers. The DES recognized that the success of their work would hinge in part upon their capacity to learn. This may be why, when the elementary supervisors were asked sixteen months into the project, "What is puzzling you in the work that you are trying to do now to support principals?," three of them said that they were puzzled by how to create more time to learn together:

> **Supervisor 1:** We need more time to plan and learn together, unpacking real-time data.
> **Supervisor 2:** How to have more time to reflect on work we are doing and make adjustments.
> **Supervisor 3:** We need more time to learn together and calibrate, balanced with planning time. Where can we get this time without being interrupted at our weekly meetings with others' agendas?

Over the two years that we worked together, we developed ways to document and learn in and from this work. Our collective capacity to closely and critically examine what we did as researchers, as practitioners, and as partners evolved and grew during this time.

A Partnership Oriented Toward Learning

As a careful observer of the DES's work, I often saw up close the myriad challenges that leading instructional improvement from the central office or from within a school entailed. Principals and district administrators talked to me about some of them. Sometimes, I had the privilege of observing intimate moments when people took risks with each other as they forged new ways of working together or addressed challenges. Other times I saw difficulties ignored or avoided. As an outsider, I occasionally noticed things that others could not easily see. Of course, the opposite was also true. As someone who was always trying to understand more deeply what was going on, I also had unique opportunities, as well as the latitude, to ask questions—some of which "insiders" might not have asked.

Sometimes these questions were consequential. For instance, when my colleagues and I noticed that many principals were not bringing "instructional problems" to the Critical Friends Conversations (CFCs), we asked the DES about this. Such questions sometimes prompted the DES to articulate out loud their thinking about what was occurring or to think more deeply about a particular situation. Making their reasoning explicit to each other or making what occurred the focus of discussion afforded the DES opportunities to scrutinize aspects of their work. Sometimes interviews did this as well. As one supervisor put it: "It's so great to have an interview and have some time to reflect, because we don't ever get this kind of time to do this at all, so thank you." Through various conversations about leading instructional improvement, the DES reconsidered and reevaluated what they were doing. Sometimes these conversations resulted in changes to their thinking and/or their actions, and sometimes they did not. Regardless, the DES felt one helpful function of our role was "to maintain the focus of their work."

MAINTAINING A FOCUS ON LEARNING AND INSTRUCTIONAL LEADERSHIP

In our DBIR role, we helped maintain the focus of the DES's work in several important ways. One was by establishing conditions to support the elementary supervisors' learning. We attended to the four context dimensions—the purpose, participants, content, and activity structure—that the instructional capacity building (ICB) framework proposes matter for learning when we led the DES's retreats, when we designed and led an institute for school instructional leadership teams, and, in a more modest way, when we participated in their regular meetings each month.

A second way we helped the DES maintain a focus on their own learning and the learning of principals was by bringing particular examples of practice (i.e., the content) into those settings and by structuring the manner in which the DES interacted with those examples. These examples from the DES's work—sometimes referred to as artifacts or records of practice—might be video recordings of an ISV debrief, examples of the problems of practice that principals brought to the CFCs, or field notes from our observations of a principal meeting or CFC. These artifacts of practice that we constructed gave the DES three different vantage points from which to view instructional leadership: macro, micro, and meso perspectives. For example, the macro perspective of instructional leadership that we offered was a conceptual map that identified places in the district system to carry out acts of instructional leadership. We also provided several micro perspectives on the DES's work that enabled the supervisors to look inside the learning structures they created and see up close what sort of learning experiences they created for principals. This micro view often honed in on specific decisions and facilitation moves that supervisors made (for instance, by examining video clips of the DES facilitating a principal conversation about classroom observations) so that they could discuss what they did that either afforded or constrained opportunities for principals to learn.

Last, we provided the DES with meso perspectives by supplying views of instructional leadership actions that principals took in their schools. For example, we documented instructional improvement episodes in a small sample of district schools. We also developed small measures of principals' self-reported leadership actions that we collectively agreed were levers for culture change in CUSD schools and were indicators of principals leading instructional improvement.[10] We also provided school instructional leadership teams with tools and routines to support leading instructional improvement in their schools. These various within-school views of instructional leadership helped the DES to see the challenges of leading instructional improvement from the vantage point of a school principal, as well as to discern the various leadership capacities that principals must possess to lead instructional change.

THE COMPLEX WORK OF LEADING DISTRICTWIDE INSTRUCTIONAL IMPROVEMENT

As actors at each level of the system undertook the complicated and demanding work of instructional improvement, various learning needs emerged across the system.

- Teachers must learn how to identify and meet particular student learning needs.
- Principals must identify what teachers need to learn in order to teach students more effectively, and then facilitate that learning.
- District administrators (working in concert across departments) have to determine what principals need to learn in order to lead instructional improvement in their schools, and then support principals' learning.

All of this needed learning requires coordinated action and interdependence across people who must do the actual work of improving teaching and student learning. These people are located at different levels of the system and typically work in isolation from each other. Thus, from the vantage point of any particular role within the district (e.g., teacher, principal, human resource administrator), it is quite difficult to get a bird's-eye view of the system as a whole, to notice how the various parts of the system might need to work together differently to coordinate their efforts, or to identify places where efforts to improve instruction vary considerably and figure out how to reduce that variability. For these reasons, we created a conceptual map. It proved helpful because it gave a more elaborate, multilevel depiction of where the work of leading instructional improvement resided within the district, who was responsible at that level, and which activities might meaningfully connect decision makers across levels of the system.

The Conceptual Map: "Seeing the Work"

The "Seeing the Work" graphic in figure 7.1 shows four levels of decision maker: district supervisors, principals, teachers, and students. Each decision maker sits adjacent to another decision maker; they are joined by an

FIGURE 7.1   *Enactment of CFCs as mapped on the resource use spectrum*

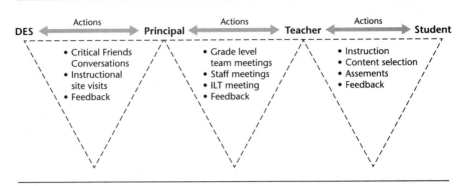

activity triangle. The triangles define some of the spaces where acts of instructional leadership can occur. They also make visible potential intersections between the levels of the system where actors from different levels can work together. The activity triangles indicate contexts where joint work to improve instruction might take place. In addition to the classroom, other contexts are specific types of school meetings (located in the triangle joining the teacher and principal) and CFCs and ISVs (in the triangle connecting principals to district supervisors). An activity triangle not depicted here might link the DES to the research team in settings like the DES's retreats.

The depicted triangles show contexts at different levels of the system. Each activity triangle is distinct and intended to evoke the instructional triangle of the classroom or the context for learning that the ICB framework defines. Magdalene Lampert has described and deconstructed the instructional triangle within classrooms to show the dynamic relationships that exist between teacher, student, and content.[11] She describes the complexity of teaching by illuminating the many decisions that a teacher makes (often in the midst of teaching) in attending to the relationships between teacher and student, student and student, content and teacher, and content and student. In her book *Teaching Problems and the Problems of Teaching*, Lampert describes a teacher's complex decision making this way:

> Many problems a teacher must address to get students to learn occur simultaneously, not one after another. Because of this simultaneity,

several different problems must be addressed in a single action. And a teacher's actions are not taken independently; they are interactions with students, individually and as a group.[12]

The interdependency of actions and simultaneity of problems that arise also occur for facilitators of adult learning. Therefore, these activity triangles are referred to as *learning triangles*, in part to emphasize that the purpose, the participants, the content, and the activity structure (the context dimensions that impact learning) need to be designed for learning something in particular. The graphic suggests that a similar complex relationship exists within each learning triangle. The interlinked series of learning triangles calls attention to the importance of the relationships that exist between actors within each triangle as well as the "content" that is selected as the focus of that interaction. The interrelationships among these dimensions affect opportunities to learn in each setting.

Finally, the adjacent triangles in the graphic highlight some of the locations where points of intersection exist between levels of the system. For example, principals and elementary supervisors both participate in ISVs. These locations (activity triangles) are depicted as sites where acts of instructional leadership could, and perhaps should, occur. The gray "action" bars with bidirectional arrows call attention to the importance of the actions that these individuals take. Recall that actions are one of the three mutually influencing elements of the instructional resourcing cycle (actions, schema, and resources), as explained in part 1. If actors located at different levels of the system (e.g., district supervisors and principals) recognize their interdependence (e.g., a principal's learning that occurs during an ISV is partially dependent on the design and structure of the ISV, which is led by the district supervisor), then they might become more inclined to codesign mutually beneficial learning experiences. Remember the district supervisor in chapter 6 who realized the need "to create the structures and the safety" so that educators at various levels would be involved in naming the "right problems" and designing their solutions. Furthermore, the graphic indicates that instructional leadership actions taken at one level of the system are likely to have direct influence only on an adjacent level (e.g., what district supervisors do with principals during a principal meeting might affect how principals interact with teachers but will not directly influence how a teacher interacts with students). Any effect the DES's actions had on teaching and student learning would be indirect.

Seeing these locations where particular decision makers can influence the actions of others helped the DES identify meaningful places to look for impact of their work: for instance, principals leading instructional improvement when facilitating an instructional leadership team (ILT) meeting, a staff meeting, or a grade-level team meeting. These settings also became places where elementary supervisors realized that they might want to follow up with principals to look for evidence of enacted principal learning. As the DES considered how their actions could help principals learn, they discussed the explicit ways they wanted their actions to influence what principals did with teachers. For example, as the group discussed the structure of ISVs, DES deliberated ways that principals might follow up with their teachers and have evidence-driven conversations with teachers that centered on artifacts of their teaching practice. Furthermore, much in the way a teacher might consider how to deepen the connection between students and content, the DES began to consider ways that they could deepen the connection between principals and the content they presented. They wondered about helping principals frame more specific problems of instructional leadership practice for CFCs, and they talked about how they focused principals on specific Common Core Standards as criteria for considering the quality of tasks they observed students working on during ISVs.

After being introduced to the "Seeing the Work" graphic, the DES also began to see more clearly the arenas where principals could influence teachers as well as the sorts of actions they could encourage principals to take. One such example was developing an "agenda template" for grade-level team meetings that guided teachers to spend their time looking at samples of student work. We also used the graphic to illuminate the settings (such as CFCs and ISVs) where the DES worked with principals. We discussed how the content of those sessions was selected as well as how the learning relationships within those contexts were developed and strengthened. Cultivating learning relationships with the people the

DES were responsible for evaluating remained an enduring tension in their work.

Using the Conceptual Graphic to Help the DES See the Impact of Their Work

We directed the DES's attention to the learning triangle where the ISVs and CFCs were situated. We facilitated a conversation about these structures that focused the DES's attention on the activities principals engaged in during CFCs and ISVs and the opportunities provided for principals to learn. Taking each structure in turn, we asked, "What is it you want principals to learn from these experiences? What is it you want to see them doing in their schools as a result of participating in these experiences?" In the language of the instructional capacity building framework, these questions asked DES to articulate the purpose of these structures. The DES responded:

* To see "big instructional shifts"
* For principals to hone their ability to name what is and is not working in their classrooms
* To raise principals' awareness of the Common Core Standards

Given these learning goals—one of which was a goal for changing teacher practice—and our aim to help the DES consider the learning design of the ISV, we considered each component of the site visit structure:

* How is the problem of practice that is presented by the host principal actually formulated?
* How do the DES guide the evidence-gathering process that occurs during classroom observations at a site visit? What is the quality of the evidence that is gathered? How useful is this evidence for the DES's overall learning purpose? Are principals getting better at collecting evidence of student and teacher actions when they observe in classrooms? What makes the DES think so?
* Is there a routine for examining the gathered evidence? What is it? What sorts of sense-making processes do principals engage in? Do

the DES facilitators use the same process? *Does a shared repertoire of practice exist?*

• What do principals learn from these school visits? And how do the DES know? What principal actions might indicate if and what principals are learning?

As the DES worked through all of these questions, the complexity of the instructional site visit emerged. What the DES wanted principals to learn from the process began to come more sharply into view. In particular, the elementary supervisors realized that they needed to do more to guide principals' attention to the actions that principals could take in their own schools to make the relationship between instruction and classroom-based evidence of student learning a focus of teachers' conversation.

Our discussion, as well as the conceptual graphic, helped make the links between acts of instructional leadership at each level of the system more visible—from participating in a site visit, to leading a staff or grade-level team meeting at the school site, to seeing a particular type of instruction in classrooms. The potential intersections between various instructional leadership activities became more obvious to the DES. Where once the DES had seen their leadership activities driving specifically toward strengthening the quality of the "learning triangle" within the classroom, now they saw that they could best influence how principals supported teachers' learning. In particular, the DES began to direct principals' attention to the specific tasks that students were being asked to perform in classrooms and to involve teachers in examining these tasks for opportunities for learning.

SMALL MEASURES OF PRINCIPALS' SELF-REPORTED LEARNING AS A LEVER FOR CHANGE

The discussion at the January retreat in the first year of the project ultimately led to a short series of survey questions that we developed with the intention of asking principals to respond to these questions each month. We asked principals two questions that were intended to be levers for change as well as provide a measure of leadership improvement:

1. What, if any, actions have you taken to help teachers consider the cognitive demand of student tasks this month? Please describe.
2. What, if any, actions have you taken to help teachers (in one grade level or more) collectively examine student work for evidence of understanding this month? Please describe.

A third question asked about any obstacles that principals encountered in trying to take such actions as frequently or as intentionally as they would have liked. Initially, some of the DES were quite concerned about asking these questions because they thought most principals were not doing either. The DES did not think principals were paying attention to the types of tasks that students were doing or expecting teachers to look together at student work. After more discussion, the DES decided to try out the survey. It was presented as a tool for collective learning—which it was—not as an evaluative instrument.

The significance of giving the survey to principals was twofold. First, the survey communicated clearly and directly to the principals the sorts of actions that DES wanted to see them take. Second, the monthly repetition of the questions signaled that these leadership moves were not one-time tasks but rather required steady attention and ongoing practice. The consistency of the questions, including the opportunity to report encountered obstacles, also sent a message to principals that the DES recognized the complexity inherent in organizing meaningful learning experiences for teachers.

What the Surveys Indicated

When the surveys came back, our research team developed a set of criteria for making sense of the data. We noticed that the manner in which principals described their actions to support teachers in looking at student tasks or student work was more interesting than whether or not a principal reported taking action. While most principals reported taking such actions, some of them provided more nuanced responses that indicated how they were asking teachers to look at student tasks to discern the level of thinking required or to engage teachers in analyzing student work for evidence of student learning. For example, one principal responded: "We have reviewed K–5 writing samples according to writing rubrics and identified action steps with each teacher and conducted classroom visits." Another said, "I have had conversations at grade-level meetings regarding math implementation and in that way, pushed our thinking around lesson planning and [our use of] questioning strategies." A third said, "We are just now starting to do this. We are in the process of collecting opinion writing in grade-level clusters. We will come together in a week to analyze student writing using the district rubrics."

The principals who provided these more nuanced descriptions also usually indicated other ways that they were creating school-based conditions to support teachers' instructional improvement. For example, one principal wrote, "Our instructional leadership team is reading *Instructional Rounds in Education*. We have been looking at student work regularly using a protocol. We are developing teacher leadership and they are planning next year's professional development." Another said, "Our work groups are trying out math tasks together." Taken together, these responses from principals indicate how they were working on improving instruction in their schools. This collection of answers stands apart as substantively different from the principals who wrote things like, "I sit in on grade-level team meetings" or "I shared positive takeaways from the instructional site visit with my staff."

The surveys also provided rich information about some of the obstacles that principals were confronting. By May in the first year of the study, time was no longer the most frequently mentioned obstacle. Instead, principals reported their own lack of knowledge as the greatest impediment to engaging teachers in this sort of work (48%); second was knowing how to structure teachers' time for learning (40%). When principals reported wanting to know more about how to facilitate teachers' learning, they asked for "more coaching strategies" for working with teachers and they wanted "to learn other metrics to measure student learning." Some wanted to know how to "establish a trusting relationship to share student work" or "how to structure time for collaboration" or "how to facilitate grade-level team meetings or professional development and provide meaningful follow-up." A few principals also expressed a desire for more support at their site to lead this work. One said, "I pray every day for a coach to help me promote the quality of grade-level collaboration." And another wanted an "an instructional coach to facilitate group and team meetings to develop inquiry questions and focus on increasing student talk with evidence." From principals' responses to these monthly survey questions, it appeared that principals were actively thinking about how to create the conditions in their schools to look carefully at what students were being asked to do and what they were learning as a result. It also appeared that for many principals, their reported actions represented new ways of leading in their schools.

LOOKING INSIDE THE STRUCTURES INTENDED FOR PRINCIPAL LEARNING

One elementary supervisor had this idea: "Let's actually look at what happens inside of an instructional leadership team meeting . . . or video how we're leading a school visit and watch it together." This desire paved the way for our research team to document episodes of the DES's enacted instructional leadership and then allow the supervisors to examine these episodes in order to learn from them. The DES's agreement to have their work documented for the purpose of strengthening their own leadership marked a significant turning point in their work; in this moment the DES made a serious commitment to learn in and from their work. In real time, this "moment" was drawn out. At first it took a while for all the supervisors to agree to be videotaped. The supervisor who was committed to the idea from the outset encouraged the others. After the first year of the study, this administrator said, "We've shifted from lots of design-oriented conversations just building structures, to thinking about the quality of the interactions inside of those structures."

A Glimpse of Principals' Instructional Leadership

We also began to identify principals who were willing to be audio or video recorded while leading instructional improvement for the purpose of helping the DES, as well as themselves, become better at this skill. These opportunities to capture instructional leadership, often in its most experimental forms, as it was unfolding provided important and unique opportunities for learning. These records of instructional leadership practice became the "content" of DES retreats and shaped the content of summer institutes held for school instructional leadership teams.

This content was connected to the DES's belief that good things invariably come out of looking closely at the work. Our role as researchers enabled us to create these records of practice, select meaningful slices of those records to show the DES, and then facilitate a learning conversation among the DES about what they noticed in the enacted leadership practices. According to one supervisor, "Getting the work on the table enables this kind of inspection and dialogue that you cannot get to if everything is entirely anecdotal." A strong belief in the value of seeing examples of actual work by some supervisors and by the research team led the DES to use its retreats to look at examples of supervisors leading principals and of principals leading teachers. As one elementary supervisor said, "It's that looking at student work process that can lead to such growth for teachers. It's not only student work, it's every form of work, when it's made public and visible and there's enough safety that you can talk about it and discuss questions of quality. Invariably, good things come out of it."

The desire that the DES had to look more closely at its enacted leadership and its impact also shaped the manner in which we engaged in our fieldwork. As is typical of a DBIR approach, a reciprocal and mutually influencing relationship formed between the researchers and the practitioners.

Inside an Instructional Site Visit Debrief

A team of two elementary administrators facilitated approximately twenty instructional site visits. The ISV protocol included setting expectations for the group, discussing the host principal's problem of practice, visiting classrooms, and finally leading a "debrief" discussion in which all participants reflected on the classroom observations and offered feedback to the host principal on the problem presented. During these debriefs, the DES experienced firsthand what it was like to facilitate an evidence-based discussion about instruction—a routine they wanted principals to adopt at their own sites. The DES discovered that facilitating these discussions often entailed challenges. For example, they had to decide how to respond to principals who were quick to judge the quality of the teaching they had seen and who commented on what the teacher could have done better.

The elementary supervisors adopted different approaches to facilitating these conversations. As with the CFC structure, some supervisors adhered closely to the ISV protocol; others only followed it loosely. Some led open-ended discussions in which principals took turns volunteering their observations; others were directive in their approach and steered principals' observations toward specific realizations about the relationship between the approach to teaching and the sort of learning opportunities that the approach afforded. Aware of these differences, we chose thin slices from the video clips of the supervisors facilitating classroom observation debriefs. We selected examples that represented their varied approaches and presented these clips at the DES retreat. Reminding the DES of the opportunity for collective learning that watching their facilitation afforded us all, we posed these prompts to frame their viewing of the videos and the discussion that followed:[13]

- What do you see or hear in this segment?
- What do you think is going on? What do you see that makes you say that?
- What insights or questions come up for you about the structure and/or facilitation of site visits?

These prompts were intentionally worded to direct the viewer to make specific claims about what was going on that were substantiated with evidence from the videos (e.g., what do you see that makes you say that?). We intended these prompts to model a simple evidence-based conversation routine that we thought the DES might want to replicate in their ISV debriefs. After viewing the clips, the DES engaged in a discussion about what they saw going on for principals and what they observed in each other's facilitation of these debriefs.

In one clip, a supervisor is shown trying to refocus a conversation among principals that was moving off-topic, away from a discussion of the student task and toward a school culture question about using talk-based approaches to mathematics instruction with Chinese bilingual students:

> **Principal:** Can I ask a cultural piece about this, because I'm noticing the last two classrooms are both Chinese bilingual, and we have a large Chinese population at our school. A lot of them go to Chinese school on the weekends and there is that expectation that you pick it up . . . the idea is about getting your answer right. So, I'm wondering how culture intersects with what you guys observed in those two classrooms and how you could see . . . how we with a Chinese demographic work on that shift [toward talk-based math instruction]?
>
> **Supervisor:** Let's keep that question . . . I think we may find that we'll be circling back to it, but very good point. Can someone talk a little bit more about the task, like what were the students asked to do and maybe the cognitive level of that?

The DES discussed the clip. A supervisor observed that one principal was trying to understand how Chinese culture was influencing what was happening in the classroom. Another supervisor noted that a different principal questioned "how open-ended" the four different ways of solving a math problem were since each approach was prescribed for the students. The supervisor added in agreement with the principal, "The students were not invited to bring their own creativity to solve the problem." A third supervisor said, "I saw the facilitator acknowledge what a principal had said, but then redirect to an analysis of the student task." These supervisor observations led another colleague to ask, "Is the facilitator aware of where he/she wants the conversation to go? And, is the facilitator asking the right questions that lead folks to focus on what's important about the lesson?"

Shortly afterward, that question was put directly to the supervisor whose facilitation they watched in the clip: "So, what were you thinking?" This supervisor explained why she had asked the question that she did: "I wanted to focus first on what principals saw in the visit. What was the cognitive demand of the [student] task?" As the DES further discussed this clip, they realized that it illuminated a moment of facilitator decision making. This realization led them to discuss the challenges inherent in facilitating these particular conversations. Another supervisor, who had not yet spoken up, said:

> In watching that, you see how hard it is to facilitate these conversations in terms of: Do principals at this point really understand what the conversation is that they should be having? And I don't think they do, at least when I facilitate. They're having this conversation *here*, and I'm trying to get them to have *this* conversation around the task. And they want to have the very important conversation about the culture, but you have to point out that *this* is why we're doing this work, this is why we're having these conversations.

This supervisor revealed that one purpose of the debriefs was to focus principal's attention on noticing the level of thinking demanded by the task that students were engaged in, which she also saw her colleague doing in this video clip. Yet, this supervisor acknowledged the difficulty of keeping principals' attention on the task, especially when principals want to talk about other matters less closely connected to teaching (e.g., choice of instructional task) and perhaps more closely linked to leading a school (e.g., parents' perception of the math curriculum).

The supervisor's rhetorical question, "Do principals at this point really understand what the conversation is that they should be having?" was directed at the moment in the clip when one principal does not take up the question about the student task but instead asks a question about the cultural values of the parents. This supervisor's comment brought into question what the learning goal was and also implied that the DES had a common learning goal for these discussions. In fact, DES had not named a specific learning goal for these conversations. Articulating a clear (and shared) learning goal can help DES make better in-the-moment decisions when facilitating such a conversation.

In another clip, a supervisor was shown interacting with a small group of principals; he was facilitating a debrief of a mathematics lesson and trying to get the group to consider, based on what they saw, the extent to which students had been offering elaborate justifications for their answers.

One principal offered his take on the lesson, describing his observation of a single student, and her failure to elaborate on her answer:

> I focused on a table where there were two boys and a girl, and the girl did something but the boys disagreed and . . . she had to reexplain how she got the number. I think she was trying to multiply two-digit numbers, and she was like, "I'll just say 125," because she couldn't really convince [the boys] because she didn't have the ability to break apart the number mentally.

Upon viewing this clip, one supervisor was struck by how much facilitation would be required to leverage a principal's reflection on a single student's thinking into actionable strategies that could lead to schoolwide improvement. This supervisor commented:

> [The facilitation] was aimed in the exactly right place in the sense that it was about the quality of children learning as evidenced by what principals saw and heard. But to get to the place where you say, all right, in this interaction, the child provides a one-word answer. That's the child's only evidence of learning . . . so what would it have sounded like if the girl had actually offered an explanation of her thinking, and then what would the lesson have been like, had she had *that* opportunity. You want to back out from evidence and strategy, but . . . that's a lot of facilitation steps for just an individual!

Here, we see the supervisor noticing the facilitation move that was used by his colleague. He wonders what other facilitation moves might have furthered the principals' thinking about what the teacher could have done to help the student provide an explanation of her thinking. What thinking led the student to select "125" as her answer? This is what the supervisor means by "you want to back out from evidence." In other words, if the student can provide only a one-word answer to describe how she approached solving this math problem, can the principal imagine what a richer answer might have been and what the teacher could have done to coax such a response from the student? Finally, does the principal know what to say to the teacher to help her consider how to expand her own instructional moves in such a situation? All of these needed facilitation moves are what led this district supervisor to conclude, "That's a lot of facilitation steps." The supervisors agreed with their colleague's thinking. One remarked that facilitating this "backing out from evidence to strategy" was a particularly great challenge considering the large number of principals attending an ISV.

Facilitating Learning

Attention to the nuanced challenges inherent in facilitating others' learning continued to surface throughout the DES's discussion of the other clips. They discovered that, with ISVs consisting of so many brief classroom observations, there seemed to be too much terrain to cover when debriefing them all. One administrator remarked how challenging it was for him to decide when it would be safe, or fruitful, to intervene in principals' conversations, in order to push against their thinking or push principals further as they reflected on observations of teachers' practice. These facilitation decisions are analogous to the ones principals must make as they lead instructional conversations among teachers at their own sites. By beginning to name these challenges, the DES took steps toward recognizing the practices embedded in facilitating a good discussion: identifying a clear learning goal for the conversation, framing the purpose of the conversation; knowing what content to select and focus on; knowing when to interject, redirect, or just listen; and knowing how to examine the evidence and then back out from the evidence to develop a strategy for doing something in particular.

Another supervisor, when reflecting on his own facilitation of a debrief involving a principal's use of grade-level team meetings, remarked that facilitating the conversation was difficult because of the sheer "range in the room" when it came to principals' ability to think about how to make use of school structures to support teachers' learning. This supervisor's insight revealed to the DES an area of knowledge for leading instructional improvement—how to strategically use school structures like grade-level team meetings, staff meetings, and instructional leadership team meetings—that principals needed to have in order to create the conditions in their schools that could help teachers learn how to adjust their instruction. Many CUSD principals lacked this particular instructional leadership knowledge. The DES needed to help principals develop this knowledge and the accompanying leadership practices.

After the clips had been discussed, a researcher asked: "What are the implications from our discussion for next year's instructional site visits?" One by one, supervisors shared suggestions for adapting the structure of the ISV: having principals view only one classroom; having more conversation with the host principals in advance of the visit, particularly the formulation of their problem of practice; and having more structured approaches for following up after the visits to ascertain whether host principals were pursuing any of the actions or ideas generated with their peers.

Reflecting on the challenges of facilitating a site visit, as well as how one might improve upon its structure, provided a learning opportunity for the DES. By opening themselves up to the experience of having inquiry-based conversations about their own work, they developed their capacity for social learning. They asked questions. They disagreed. They listened to each other's perspectives. They experienced feeling vulnerable. They also named and agreed upon a purpose for the ISV debriefs. They identified problems with the ISV's current structure—too many classrooms observed in a visit to discuss and no guarantee about the quality of the instruction in the observed classroom. Another concern was the difficulty of following up with principals after they had hosted an ISV to learn how they were using the experience to influence future leadership actions. The DES's examination of this issue led them to make some changes to the ISV structure the following year. For instance, the DES linked the ISV and Critical Friends structure so principals could report specific actions they took to address their presented problem of practice; the DES also reduced the number of classrooms observed during ISVs. These collectively agreed-upon changes are indicators that the DES viewed the ISVs and CFCs as a joint enterprise. In year two, DES began to further develop a shared set of practices for using these structures to help principals learn.

Constraints to Learning

A limitation of our video debrief exercise was that it did not create sufficient opportunities for the DES to explicitly consider what principals might do, or do differently, as a result of having hosted an ISV. In the video clips, the DES saw ISV debriefs that revolved around what principals had observed: principals discussed teachers' lessons and instructional tasks, critiquing them on their level of cognitive demand and their alignment with the Common Core Standards. However, it soon became apparent that influencing an individual teacher's moment-by-moment instructional choices was not within a principal's locus of control as an instructional leader. Rather, what the principal could influence was the creation and facilitation of new structures that would help teachers to think differently about their instruction, a goal that remained somewhat elusive for the DES as they watched the videos.

As the group watched another video, in which two supervisors proposed shifts in the way a school conducted its grade-level team meetings, the most salient takeaway for the DES was that their colleague was "doing what he does best"—being directive and taking charge, and telling principals exactly what their next steps should be. What was not explicitly named during the discussion, however, was that this facilitation move offered the host principal a way he could lead instructional improvement at his school. In other words, the facilitator proposed that the group consider the use of the grade-level team to better structure the ambiguous problem of leading instructional improvement, naming the grade-level team meeting as a structure within that principal's locus of control, and identifying that context as a potentially constructive place to hold meaningful conversations about instruction grounded in practice-based evidence. Once the grade-level team meeting was identified for this purpose, many principals still needed to learn how to structure grade-level meetings for meaningful teacher learning. As chapters 3 and 4 describe, principals do not necessarily know how to create these conditions inside of these school structures.

Through their analysis of ISVs, the DES began to develop shared ideas about the knowledge that principals needed to lead instructional improvement in their schools. Principals needed to establish an instructional leadership team as well as use the existing structures within their school—the grade-level team meetings and the weekly staff meetings—as places where they could guide teachers' instructional approach and cultivate practices of closely and collaboratively examining student work to identify student misunderstandings and to design instructional next steps.

LOOKING AT WHAT HAPPENS INSIDE SCHOOLS

To help the DES get a different view of how instructional leadership occurs inside of schools, we also shared portraits of CUSD instructional leadership practice. The school portraits of enacted instructional leadership were developed from typical problems that we witnessed when we spent time in the schools. For example, one portrait showed a veteran principal's insecurity and vulnerability as she talked with teachers about changing the structure and purpose of grade-level team meetings. This principal wanted to reclaim control of the grade-level meetings at her school and do away with what in her words had become "chit-chat and teacher talk time." This principal viewed teachers' current use of these meetings as "the biggest waste of time." The grade-level meeting time was not used for looking at student work, designing instruction, or in other ways collaborating on matters of teaching and learning. This principal, however, needed help to figure out how to engage teachers in a constructive conversation about the reason to alter the use of this time.

Looking back, the principal recalled, "My biggest problem was some of these barriers that [teachers] were putting up. . . . I needed to get the teachers to trust me." The portrait of this principal struggling with how to frame a conversation about refocusing the use of grade-level team time at her school caught the DES's attention, particularly because this was an experienced and well-thought-of principal. One supervisor said, "That's the leadership piece people struggle with. . . . Some principals want to just set up the structures and then be able to walk way. We need to help principals understand how important it is for them to be part of teachers' conversations." This supervisor noted how different the teacher conversation often became when the principal was not present, and she drew upon a recent experience in which she observed several teacher teams meeting, some with and others without the principal, to make her point. The DES wanted to know how they could help principals prioritize supporting teachers' instructional conversations or help them manage the competing demands on their time so that they don't step away from these teacher conversations.

Inside an Instructional Leadership Team Meeting

Another portrait we offered DES was a video clip of an instructional leadership team (ILT) composed of teachers, an instructional coach, and the school principal discussing a video clip they had just watched of a teacher from their school (who was also taking part in the ILT discussion) leading a literature discussion with his fourth-grade class. We introduced this clip to the DES as a way to see "the work that principals are doing with teachers." Working in partnership with this principal, we had facilitated the ILT's conversation about their colleague's lesson. We brought this example of instructional leadership to the DES because it represented a less familiar way of leading instructional improvement in schools. As the DES watched the discussion among a group of school educators, they saw an example of how a teacher's instructional expertise could be recorded, shared with staff, and used as a resource to prompt focused discussion about effective instruction, what counts as evidence of student learning, and teacher facilitation moves during a student discussion. The DES not only saw how this resource was used with a school instructional leadership team, they also heard the sorts of conversations that the video clip prompted and saw how staff members engaged with this resource.

In their discussion, the DES observed the important role that facilitation played during the ILT discussion. One supervisor made this realization: "I haven't ever given [this particular principal] feedback on how she leads a meeting, and yet that's so important." The DES realized that providing principals with feedback on their design and facilitation of staff meetings was a practice missing from their own leadership. A connection was also made to principals' request for help with how to structure and facilitate teachers' collaborative conversations. The DES recalled the small-measure principal survey and realized many principals had asked for just this sort of help. The DES's discussion led another supervisor to conclude: "There lies the focus of principals' meetings: how to teach principals how to lead their ILT and give them feedback." Another supervisor wondered, "How do we provide feedback to the principal and the ILT about how they are functioning? This is a point of leverage that we may have overlooked, especially for low-performing schools . . . . We need to create our own structure for visiting the ILT meetings."

As the DES listened to and discussed the comments that the ILT participants made about their colleague's teaching, they also noticed some knowledge gaps among the school coaches, in particular the coach's capacity to recognize effective instructional moves. The DES's close examination of the video led the DES to again comment on the intrinsic value of having educators conduct a close inspection of practice focused on the relationship between teaching and learning. Such conversations they thought "were unusual." Together they wondered what it would take to have such conversations become commonplace in CUSD schools.

After considering these episodes of leading instructional improvement in schools grounded in concrete records of practices, the DES created a detailed list of specific actions that instructional leaders (both principals and district administrators) could take when working on improving instruction. Included on the list were: select and examine formative data; provide quality feedback to principals, to grade-level teams, and to teachers; and participate in grade-level team conversations about student learning with teachers. They also generated some questions about their own leadership work rooted in areas where they noticed principals needed more support.

- How can we support principals in building site-based capacity for stronger grade-level team meetings and ILT meetings?
- How can we help principals "reorganize their thinking" about how to engage teachers in looking at student work?
- How can we help principals develop a strong learning climate in their schools?

Their questions were specific but big. They were grounded in the sort of support the DES now realized principals needed. While the DES did not have all the solutions, they had become much more specific about what principals needed to know and learn to do. The DES's more nuanced understanding of principals' learning needs enabled them to make some significant adjustments to how they designed principal learning structures the following year. On the spectrum of resource use, the DES had figured out how to adjust the resource (such as the ISV and CFC) to better fit the learning needs of principals and was therefore likely to become better able to develop principals' capacity for leading instructional improvement.

SUMMARY

As outsiders, researchers can collect or develop a wide array of records of practice, select meaningful episodes from those records, and then design a structured approach for collaborative analysis of those episodes by practitioners. Researchers can also facilitate these conversations, making sure that the learning environment remains a safe place so that learning can occur. Researchers can model evidence-based talk and the instructive potential of asking probing questions. By engaging in such joint practices with other educators, researchers can help practitioners (district administrators, principals, coaches, or teachers) develop their own routines for examining their own practice. Through such experiences, as the accounts in this chapter indicate, participants may alter their thinking (i.e., schema), take different actions, and/or identify new resources to support future learning. These new resources might be any type of instructional resource—relationships, structures, routines, tools and materials, or knowledge—that comes from gaining insight and a deeper understanding. Thus researchers, when purposefully involved in practitioners' work, can assume an important role in accelerating practitioners' efforts to increase their capacity for instructional leadership and improvement.

THE PURSUIT OF INSTRUCTIONAL CAPACITY

B uilding instructional capacity for continuous learning improvement is portrayed in this book as an ongoing collective effort. Though this work is complex, the educators at Cedar Bridge and the administrators in the Coopersville Union School District have demonstrated *how* to do it. Knowing what instructional capacity is and how it develops helps focus our attention on the actions the individuals in these settings take, such as identifying particular instructional resources, articulating a clear purpose for their use, and examining the effects of using these resources. We are able to see how well the use of the resource is connected to a learning goal as well as to the user's learning needs.

The instructional capacity building framework gives us a lens through which to examine the differences between the teacher conversations that occurred at Cedar Bridge and Liberty as well as a way to understand the different actions of the two principals. The Liberty principal accumulated instructional resources, while the Cedar Bridge principal invested in learn-ing how to use a few resources well. The concept of instructional capacity can also help explain the conditions under which particular resources get used. For instance, ideas about how instructional capacity grows help to explain how a Cedar Bridge teacher, Molly, developed her ability over time to use a particular reading strategy and why a Liberty teacher, Will, perceived right away that this strategy was a valuable approach to teaching. The concept of how to increase instructional capacity also suggests possible actions that could be taken to help another Liberty teacher, Pat, begin to use these reading strategies in her teaching.

The collection of examples in this book also shows that creating the conditions for learning and developing capacity for instructional improvement require changing the norms, practices, and social organization of schooling at every level. Yet we see that the levels of the system are often disconnected from one another. We also see educators (teachers, principals, district administrators) typically working in isolation with relatively few learning supports, like the administrators in CUSD and the teachers at Liberty—even though Liberty teachers had a bountiful supply of instructional tools and materials and regular time to meet. Ideas of instructional capacity building propose ways to reduce this isolation through the meaningful use of resources and by creating connections with others located in different roles and in different parts of the system.

THE IMPERATIVE OF EXPANDING A SYSTEM'S CAPACITY FOR LEARNING

Creating these cross-level and cross-role connections is essential for developing the system's capacity to support high-quality learning, as the work of educators in this book shows. Classrooms, schools, and districts have become increasingly demanding places in which to lead instructional improvement. Therefore, a collective approach to the work of building instructional capacity is needed now more than ever. The increased accountability policies and pressures that district administrators, principals, and teachers must work under today, the challenges of educating historically underserved populations of students to higher standards, and high teacher and principal turnover rates—a problem that is compounded by the shortage of well-prepared teachers and principals entering the field— combine to make leading instructional improvement difficult. Add to these demands the more ambitious expectations for student learning brought by the Common Core Standards and the new, commensurate forms of assessment (e.g., the Smarter Balanced assessments and other performance assessments), and the enormity, as well as the urgency, of the instructional and instructional leadership challenges come sharply into view.

Given the magnitude and complexity of the task, it is imperative that educators approach developing conditions for learning at each level of the system as a collective undertaking and view the work as shared and interdependent. The stories of Cedar Bridge and Liberty middle schools provide educative and contrasting cases in this regard. The organizational conditions and features of the social learning context in these two schools differed dramatically, not because the collaborative structures within the schools were so different, but because of how the collaborative work was organized and supported within those structures. The nature of the supports that teachers received, which was influenced by the principal's actions and beliefs about how teachers best learn, differed in crucial ways. Importantly, at Cedar Bridge, supporting teachers' collaborative work was approached as a collective and interdependent effort. At Liberty, it was not.

COMMON APPROACHES FOR BUILDING INSTRUCTIONAL CAPACITY

Precisely what building instructional capacity for continuous instructional improvement looks like across levels of the educational system—in classrooms and within schools, between schools within a district, and within the central office—differs. Part 2 of this book has provided some examples of how to create conditions for learning throughout the system. Looking across these chapters, we can see that common approaches to expanding instructional capacity do exist. Following is a brief summary of these approaches.

Identify Important Problems of Practice

Problems of practice occur at every level of the educational system. Teachers, principals, and district administrators all need the ability to notice problematic aspects of how they conduct their work—whether learning, teaching, or leading—that if improved, are likely to make a significant difference for student learning. This is the practice of "problem setting" that we saw Cedar Bridge engage in as part of its process for identifying resources; it is also the process that led CUSD district administrators to design, use, and refine their principal meeting structures by introducing the Critical Friends Conversations and the instructional site visits. Educators may need support to identify their problems of practice, to determine which problems are most important to resolve, and to frame the context in which to work on resolving them. Identifying problems of practice is step one. Determining their significance for improving student learning is step two. Understanding the problem well enough to begin developing a strategy to resolve it is step three.

Educational workplaces ought to be organized in a way that helps practitioners identify important problems worthy of their time and realize actions to take to begin solving them. Think about the conversations that the humanities teachers at Cedar Bridge had with one another or the discussions that the elementary supervisors had with individual principals in preparation for the Critical Friends Conversations, or the principal conversations that were structured by the CFCs. Each of these structures represents an attempt (some more successful than others) to help educators see their own work and its effects more clearly.

Determine the Problem's Significance in Relation to Improving Student Learning Opportunities

Problems related to learning, teaching, and leading abound in education, so it's critical to select the most important ones to work on. To strengthen capacity for high-quality teaching, we need to focus collective attention on the problems of practice that are most likely to influence the quality of students' learning experiences. Principal Seymore Everett at Cedar Bridge acted in accordance with this idea when he and his colleagues introduced professional learning communities to develop teachers' capacity to examine student learning and better guide instructional decisions. The district elementary supervisors adhered to this idea when they decided to focus principals' attention on problems related to leading instructional improvement rather than on other aspects of leading, such as managerial or operational problems.

Develop Opportunities to Better Understand the Problem of Practice

Problems of practice are best explored, as well as recognized in the first place, by having regular opportunities to examine practice. One good way to create the conditions for learning is to develop opportunities where the practice of educators (e.g., the work of teaching, including lessons, tasks, and assessments; and acts of leading, such the DES's facilitation of the principals' ISVs and CFCs) is made available for examination, inquiry, and discussion for the purpose of learning and improving that practice. When the practice itself becomes the object of study and investigation, then a shared understanding of that practice, in addition to a repertoire for practicing well, can begin to develop. This book is full of such examples of educators looking together at the work of students, teachers, principals, and administrators.

These examples also show that conducting such examinations of practice in a meaningful manner is challenging. Having external partners to engage with practitioners, as described in chapter 7, may be helpful. Conversations about the practice need to be well structured, and the quality of the deliberation honed. Providing feedback to participants, as the Cedar Bridge leadership team did and as the research team did for the DES, is also a helpful strategy. Keep in mind the learning purpose as well as the learning needs of the participants who are engaged in the conversation. These two dimensions of the spectrum of resource use can help when selecting the activity structure, tools, or routines to use during these examinations of practice as well as when trying to determine how effective the process was and what adjustments are needed.

Define a Clear Learning Goal and a Way to Measure Progress

The reason to develop instructional capacity is to achieve something in particular, not simply to amass capacity. At Cedar Bridge, we saw that a learning goal for teachers was to develop their ability to closely examine student performance for evidence of learning and then to design instruction specifically to help students who were not learning well enough, especially African American students. The use of instructional resources at Cedar Bridge was aimed at helping teachers to develop these specific capacities. The measures of learning that Cedar Bridge leaders created were the meeting notes as well as classroom visits. In CUSD, we saw that district administrators had a learning goal for elementary principals: to become more capable leaders of instructional improvement in their schools. The DES introduced various changes to principal meetings intended to develop principals' abilities to that end. It was evident that keeping the use of these structures aligned to that specific goal was difficult amid competing priorities, external pressures, and emerging problems. We also saw that designing useful measures of principals' progress toward this goal required articulating what leading instructional improvement in schools actually entailed.

Identify and Use All Available Instructional Assets

Building instructional capacity requires having and using the four types of instructional resources—instructional knowledge, instructional technology, instructionally oriented relationships, and organizational structures. The examples in this book have shown that once a problem of practice is identified, it is useful to consider all of the possible assets that might help solve that particular problem. Often, making noticeable progress toward a solution involves changing one's conception about how to approach the problem (such as altering the purpose of teacher collaboration at Cedar Bridge or changing the purpose of principal meetings in CUSD). Also, working toward a solution often involves a different use of existing resources. For example, this happened in CUSD when the district elementary supervisors began to work together to design, lead, and ultimately strengthen the learning that occurred during principal meetings. In addition, the DES's different conception of the purpose of principal meetings led the supervisors to identify assets for principal learning that were previously unrecognized as such—for example, classroom instruction and principals' own leadership problems. Instances of classroom instruction and the naming and framing of leadership problems became important "resources" for principal learning in the context of the supervisors' reframed conception of what principals needed to know and be able to do.

Organize for Interdependent Work

Finally, building instructional capacity within an organization requires interdependence. Organizing instructional work in ways that require educators to coordinate their actions and participate in joint decision making also helps to stimulate the development of instructional resources and instructional capacity. When work is viewed as requiring interdependence, that stimulates the creation of new ways of working together. We saw this phenomenon occur with the DES when they approached the design and facilitation of the elementary principals' meetings as interdependent work. The DES developed the CFC and ISV organizational structures and refined these routines. Or, consider the knowledge of students and of instruction that was created through the interdependent behavior of the Cedar Bridge teachers as they developed common lessons and formative assessments. When the CUSD elementary administrators and the humanities teachers at Cedar Bridge approached their work in an interdependent manner, they began to learn from each other and to develop shared (and more effective) methods for working with principals and students.

SEIZE THE OPPORTUNITY

Strengthening students' opportunities for learning in schools and districts requires the intentional and purposeful use of instructional resources. Progress toward more meaningful learning can get under way with the resources that currently exist in the setting where you work. Using these instructional resources in a meaningful way that actually leads to improved opportunities for all students to learn will generate additional resources that can be used to continue to improve learning opportunities. However, building capacity for continuous instructional improvement requires creating the conditions in our school systems for the adults to learn, too. As the examples given in this book have shown, we can get better at developing these conditions.

Improving school and district learning conditions begins with intentional action and a belief that we can improve our workplace conditions. Doing so also requires ongoing attention—paying attention to the overriding purpose for that learning, noticing what individual and collective actions we take in service of achieving that purpose, being aware of the schema and assumptions with which we operate, and recognizing how we identify and use instructional resources and to what ends. Making existing conditions more conducive to learning also requires being open to seeing situations, practices, and opportunities in new ways. Our openness to learning and attention to how well the resources in use actually fit our overall learning goals and the needs of our learners can increase capacity for improving instruction. Teachers, principals, and district administrators can make schools and districts places where meaningful learning occurs every day.

NOTES

INTRODUCTION

1. Kurt Lewin, "The Research Center for Group Dynamics at Massachusetts Institute of Technology," *Sociometry* 8, no. 2 (1945): 126–36, quoted in Andrew Van de Ven, "Nothing Is Quite So Practical as a Good Theory," *Academy of Management Review* 14, no. 4 (1989): 486–89.
2. Ann Jaquith, "The Creation and Use of Instructional Resources: The Puzzle of Professional Development" (PhD diss., Stanford University, 2009).
3. See Ann Jaquith, "Building System Instructional Leadership Capacity to Develop Effective Data Use Practices" (paper presented at the International Congress for School Effectiveness and Improvement, Santiago, Chile, January 2013); Ann Jaquith, "Developing System Capacity to Support Principals' Instructional Leadership" (paper delivered at AERA Annual Meeting, San Francisco, CA, April 2013); A. Jaquith, L. Aiello, and E. Khachatryan, "Developing District Instructional Leadership Capacity: Creating the Conditions for Learning to Lead Instructional Improvement" (paper delivered at the National Center on Scaling Up Effective Schools second national conference: Using Continuous Improvement to Integrate Design, Implementation, and Scale Up, Nashville, TN, October 2015).

CHAPTER 1

1. Bradley S. Portin et al., "Leading Learning-Focused Teacher Leadership in Urban High Schools," *Journal of School Leadership* 23, no. 2 (2013): 22.
2. Etienne Wenger, *Communities of Practice: Learning, Meaning, and Identity* (Cambridge, UK: Cambridge University Press, 1998).
3. Yrjo Engstrom and Reijo Miettinen, "Activity Theory: A Well-Kept Secret," in *Perspectives on Activity Theory*, eds. Yrjo Engstrom et al. (Cambridge, UK: Cambridge University Press, 1999), 1–16.
4. For further discussions of how organizational and sociocultural learning theories are useful for examining the problem of systemwide instructional reform in school districts, see Michael Knapp, ed., *American Educational Journal of Education* 114, no. 4 (2008).

5. Wenger, *Communities of Practice*.

6. This vignette is an excerpt from Ann Jaquith, "Instructional Capacity: How to Build It Right," *Educational Leadership* 71, no. 2 (2013): 56–61. Reprinted with permission.

7. David K. Cohen, Stephen Raudenbush, and Deborah L. Ball, "Resources, Instruction, and Research," *Educational Evaluation and Policy Analysis* 25, no. 2 (2003): 11942. For an exception, see Elizabeth City, *Resourceful Leadership* (Cambridge, MA: Harvard Education Press, 2008). City describes resources beyond time, money, and people that matter for improving teaching, such as vision, hope, trust, ideas, and energy.

8. Kathleen M. Eisenhardt and Jeffrey A. Martin, "Dynamic Capabilities: What Are They?" *Strategic Management Journal* 21, no. 10 (2000), quoted in Martha Feldman, "Resources in Emerging Structures and Processes of Change," *Organization Science* 15, no. 3 (2004): 295.

9. Feldman, "Resources in Emerging Structures and Processes of Change," 295–309.

10. Everett M. Rogers, *Diffusion of Innovations* (New York: Simon and Schuster, 2010), 13.

11. Ibid.

12. In Wenger's terms, the sticky notes are what reifies this instructional method into "thingness."

13. Lee Shulman's construct of pedagogical content knowledge, for instance, discriminates between having subject-matter knowledge and using subject-matter knowledge for instruction. See Lee Shulman, "Knowledge and Teaching: Foundations of the New Reform," *Harvard Educational Review* 57, no. 1 (1987): 1–23.

14. Joanne Martin argues that three distinct research paradigms exist in the organizational culture literature and that most organizational studies portray culture from one of these three perspectives—integration, differentiation, or fragmentation. She argues that an organization is a nexus "in which a variety of internal and external cultural influences come together . . . and interact within boundaries that are moveable, fluctuating, permeable, blurred and dangerous" (339–40). For an extended discussion of these three views of organizational culture, see Joanne Martin, *Organizational Culture: Mapping the Terrain* (Thousand Oaks: Sage Publications, 2001).

15. For a comprehensive discussion of learning-focused leadership and its distributed leadership structures, see Michael Knapp et al., *Learning-Focused Leadership in Action: Improving Instruction in Schools and Districts* (New York: Routledge, 2014).

16. Susan Rosenholtz, *Teachers' Workplace: The Social Organization of Schools* (New York: Addison-Wesley Longman, 1989).

17. Knapp, *Learning-Focused leadership*; Viviane Robinson, Claire A. Lloyd, and Kenneth J. Rowe, "The Impact of Leadership on Student Outcomes: An Analysis of the Differential Effects of Leadership Types," *Educational Administration Quarterly* 44, no. 5 (2008): 635–74.

18. Anthony Bryk and Barbara Schneider, *Trust in Schools: A Core Resource for Improvement* (New York: Russell Sage Foundation, 2002).

19. Ibid., 13, 33.

20. Ibid., 23.

21. Rosenholtz, *Teachers' Workplace*.

22. Feldman, "Resources in Emerging Structures."

23. Ibid., 297, emphasis added.

24. Thomas Guskey, "Staff Development and the Process of Teacher Change," *Educational Researcher* 15, no. 5 (1986): 5–12.

25. Richard C. Anderson, Rand J. Spiro, and William E. Montague, *Schooling and the Acquisition of Knowledge* (Hillsdale, NJ: Lawrence Erlbaum Associates, 1977), 425.

26. A body of research in the field of teacher learning documents the difficulty of altering teachers' schema for teaching particular bodies of knowledge. For examples, see David Cohen, "A Revolution in One Classroom: The Case of Mrs. Oublier," *Educational Evaluation and Policy Analysis* 12, no. 3 (1990): 311–29; Howard Gardner, *Intelligence Reframed: Multiple Intelligences for the 21st Century* (New York: Basic Books, 1999); Judith Warren Little, "Locating Learning in Teachers' Communities of Practice: Opening Up Problems of Analysis in Records of Everyday Work," *Teaching and Teacher Education* 18, no. 8 (2002): 917–46; and Janine Remillard, "Can Curriculum Materials Support Teachers' Learning? Two Fourth-Grade Teachers' Use of New Mathematics Text," *Elementary School Journal* 100, no. 4 (2000): 331–51.

27. For a discussion of how Cedar Bridge principals came to the realization that standardized test scores were not useful, see Ann Jaquith, "Site-Based Leadership for Improving Instruction," *Educational Forum* 79, no. 1 (2015): 12–23.

28. Wenger describes this as the dual process of participation and reification; see Wenger, *Communities of Practice*, 55–58.

29. Wenger, *Communities of Practice*, 45.

30. Wenger, *Communities of Practice*; Anderson et al., *Schooling and the Acquisition of Knowledge*, 425.

31. Magdalene Lampert, *Teaching Problems and the Problems of Teaching* (New Haven, CT: Yale University Press, 2003).

32. Megan Franke and colleagues conceptualize "generativity" within teachers' learning process. See Megan Franke et al., "Capturing Teachers' Generative Change: A Follow-up Study of Professional Development in Mathematics," *American Educational Research Journal* 38, no. 3 (2001): 653–89.

33. Feldman, "Resources in Emerging Structures," 295.

34. Rogers, *Diffusion of Innovations*.

35. Karl Weik, *Sensemaking in Organizations* (Thousand Oaks, CA: Sage Publications, 1995), 9.

36. Wenger, *Communities of Practice*, 52.

37. Wenger, *Communities of Practice*, 64.

38. Donal Schon in Karl Weik, *Sensemaking*, 40.

39. For example, see Illana Horn, "Learning on the Job: A Situated Account of Teacher Learning in High School Mathematics Departments," *Cognition and Instruction* 114, no. 4 (2005); Judith Warren Little, "Inside Teacher Community: Representations of Classroom Practice," *Teachers College Record* 105, no. 6 (2003); Judith Warren Little and Illana Horn, "'Normalizing' Problems of Practice: Converting Routine Conversation into a Resource for Learning in Professional Communities," in *Professional Learning Communities: Divergence, Depth and Dilemmas*, eds. Louise Stoll and Karen Seashore Louis (Maidenhead, UK: McGraw-Hill/Open University Press, 2007), 79–92; Milbrey McLaughlin and Joan Talbert, *Professional Communities and the Work of High School Teaching* (Chicago: University of Chicago Press, 2001); and Milbrey McLaughlin and Joan Talbert, *Building School-Based Teacher Learning Communities: Professional Strategies to Improve Student Achievement* (New York: Teachers College Press, 2006).

40. Chrysan Gallucci, "Districtwide Instructional Reform: Using Sociocultural Theory to Link Professional Learning to Organizational Support," *American Journal of Education* 114, no. 4 (2008): 541–82; Mary Kay Stein and Cynthia Coburn, "Architectures for Learning: A Comparative Analysis of Two Urban School Districts," *American Journal of Education* 114, no. 4 (2008): 583–626.

41. Stein and Coburn, "Architectures for Learning," 585.

42. Stein and Coburn call this "stuff" boundary objects, connecting the reification or thingness of the reforms to Wenger's theory of communities of practice.

43. Stein and Coburn, "Architectures for Learning," 616. For a related point, also see Pamela Grossman and Clarissa Thompson, "Learning from Curriculum Materials: Scaffolds for New Teachers?," *Teaching and Teacher Education* 24, no. 8 (2008): 2014–26.

44. Stein and Coburn, "Architectures for Learning," 586.

45. For discussions of different perceptions of organizational culture, see Paul DiMaggio, "Culture and Cognition," *Annual Review of Sociology* 23, no. 1 (1997): 263–87; and Martin, *Organizational Culture*.

CHAPTER 2

1. This description of the fitting process illustrates Wenger's theory that participation in a process always involves the duality of participation and reification. For further discussion about this duality, see Etienne Wenger, *Communities of Practice: Learning, Meaning, and Identity* (Cambridge, UK: Cambridge University Press, 1998), 66–69.

2. Wenger, *Communities of Practice*, 65.

3. David K. Cohen, Stephen Raudenbush, and Deborah L. Ball, "Resources, Instruction, and Research," *Educational Evaluation and Policy Analysis* 25, no. 2 (2003): 119–42.

4. Some organizational and institutional scholars ask questions about how ideas travel within and among organizations. See Paul Carlile, "Transferring, Translating, and Transforming: An Integrative Framework for Managing Knowledge Across Boundaries," *Organization Science* 15, no. 5 (2004): 555–68; Martha S. Feldman and Brian T. Pentland. "Reconceptualizing Organizational Routines as a Source of Flexibility and Change," *Administrative Science Quarterly* 48, no. 1 (2003): 94–118; Andrew Hargadon and Robert I. Sutton, "Technology Brokering and Innovation in a Product Development Firm," *Administrative Science Quarterly* 42, no. 4 (1997): 716–49. Diffusion mechanisms are typically studied at the macro level to explain how particular structures spread and to offer explanations for why organizational structures in a particular field are often the same. For example, see Paul DiMaggio and Walter W. Powell, "The Iron Cage Revisited: Collective Rationality and Institutional Isomorphism in Organizational Fields," *American Sociological Review* 48, no. 2 (1983): 147–60; or David Strang and John W. Meyer, "Institutional Conditions for Diffusion," *Theory and Society* 22, no. 4 (1993): 487–511.

5. Wenger, *Communities of Practice*, 119.

6. Ibid., 120.

7. Ibid., 256.

8. Ibid., 112–13.

9. Ibid., 105.

10. Ibid., 105.

11. Michael L. Tushman and Thomas J. Scanlan, "Boundary Spanning Individuals: Their Role in Information Transfer and Their Antecedents," *Academy of Management Journal* 24, no. 2 (1981): 289–305; Richard W. Scott, "Institutional Carriers: Reviewing Modes of Transporting Ideas Over Time and Space and Considering Their Consequences," *Industrial and Corporate Change* 12, no. 4 (2003): 879–94.

12. Scott, "Institutional Carriers," 879.

13. Ibid., 882.

14. Ibid., 882.
15. Howard Aldrich and Diane Herker, "Boundary Spanning Roles and Organization Structure," *Academy of Management Review* 2, no. 2 (1977): 217–30; Tushman and Scanlan, "Boundary Spanning Individuals."
16. Aldrich and Herker, "Boundary Spanning Roles."
17. Aldrich and Herker, "Boundary Spanning Roles"; Carlile, "Transferring, Translating, and Transforming"; Hargadon and Sutton, "Technology Brokering"; Tushman and Scanlan, "Boundary Spanning Individuals."
18. Hargadon and Sutton's work on technology brokering in the product design and development firm IDEO is an exception. Their process model of innovation describes the generation of resources as the result of an organizational mechanism: brainstorming groups. The brokering of information in this study is intra-organizational.
19. Wesley Cohen and Daniel Levinthal describe the boundary spanning roles as functionally critical for R&D units in "Absorptive Capacity: A New Perspective on Learning and Innovation," *Administrative Science Quarterly* 35, no. 1 (1990):128–52. Boundary spanning is the mechanism that enables R&D units to develop the capacity to recognize, "absorb," and use new industry knowledge for the organization's innovation and to its advantage.
20. See Cohen and Levinthal, "Absorptive Capacity."
21. For a discussion of how an educational organization functions as an intermediary to facilitate regional school reform, see Ann Jaquith and Milbrey McLaughlin, "A Temporary Intermediary Organization at the Helm of Regional Educational Reform: Lessons from the Bay Area School Reform Collaborative," in *Second International Handbook of Educational Change*, eds. Andy Hargreaves et al. (London: Springer, 2010), 85–103.
22. Tushman and Scanlan's term is "informational boundary spanner" as distinguished from "representational" boundary spanners, who are "external communication stars" who "represent the organization externally (e.g., salesmen)" but without disseminating information within the organization.
23. Tushman and Scanlan, "Boundary Spanning Individuals," 300.
24. Ibid., 300.

CHAPTER 3

1. The four teacher portraits are drawn from a qualitative comparative case study of two schools. Data collection and analysis included observations of 43 teacher meetings; 23 classroom observations; 22 interviews with 12 focal teachers and 4 administrators; and 108 hours of professional development observations in which teachers from both schools participated.

Data collection occurred during the 2007–2008 school year. All proper names in this book are pseudonyms with the exception of the Reading Apprenticeship.

2. Reading Apprenticeship (RA) is a professional development program created by the Strategic Literacy Initiative at WestEd. For additional information, see https://readingapprenticeship.org/about-us/.

3. For a description of this approach to literacy instruction, see Ruth Schoenbach, Cynthia Greenleaf, and Lynn Murphy, *Reading for Understanding: How Reading Apprenticeship Improves Disciplinary Learning in Secondary and College Classrooms*, 2nd edition (San Francisco: Jossey-Bass, 2012).

4. For a discussion of teachers' help-seeking and help-giving behaviors, see Susan J. Rosenholtz, *Teachers' Workplace: The Social Organization of Schools* (New York: Addison-Wesley Longman, 1989).

5. Milbrey W. McLaughlin and Dana Mitra, "Theory-based Change and Change-based Theory: Going Deeper, Going Broader," *Journal of Educational Change* 2, no. 4 (2001): 301–23.

6. Ibid., 306.

7. Ibid., 306–7.

CHAPTER 4

1. Michael Knapp et al., *Learning-Focused Leadership in Action: Improving Instruction in Districts and Schools* (New York: Routledge, 2014), provides a discussion of instructional improvement.

2. Data for this chapter is drawn from the qualitative comparative case study referenced in chapter 3, note 1.

3. The name of this professional development program is a pseudonym.

4. For more on how this school thought about standardized test scores as a measure of performance, see Ann Jaquith, "Site-Based Leadership for Improving Instruction," *Educational Forum* 79, no. 1 (2015): 12–23.

5. Susan Rosenholtz, *Teachers' Workplace: The Social Organization of Schools* (New York: Addison-Wesley Longman, 1989).

6. For a complete discussion of how leaders at Cedar Bridge actually led the ongoing work of PLCs and functioned as their own PLC in order to do so, see Jaquith, "Site-Based Leadership."

7. Lorna M. Earl and Helen Timperly, "Understanding How Evidence and Learning Conversations Work," in *Professional Learning Conversations: Challenges Using Evidence for Improvement*, eds. L. M. Earl and H. Timperley (London: Springer Science + Business).

8. Jaquith, "Site-Based Leadership."

9. Teach for America website, https://www.teachforamerica.org/about-us/our -mission (retrieved 2008).

10. Dan C. Lortie, *Schoolteacher: A Sociological Study* (Chicago: University of Chicago Press, 1975), 14.

CHAPTER 5

1. This analysis draws upon a qualitative study of district elementary school supervisors and their efforts to develop principals as instructional leaders in CUSD, conducted in 2013–2015. Data in the form of relevant district documents, 27 interviews with 8 district administrators and 6 principals, and observations of 48 Critical Friend Conversations, 24 instructional site visits, 25 district administrator meetings, and 20 additional principal meetings was collected and analyzed.

2. The idea that you learn the work by doing the work is at the center of the Instructional Rounds approach, which was a practice that CUSD was concurrently experimenting with in other areas of the district. For an explanation of Instructional Rounds, see Richard F. Elmore, Sarah E. Fiarman, and Lee Teitel, *Instructional Rounds in Education: A Network Approach to Improving Teaching and Learning* (Cambridge, MA: Harvard Education Press, 2009).

CHAPTER 6

1. Joan Talbert, "Professional Learning Communities at the Crossroads: How Systems Hinder or Engender Change," in *Second International Handbook of Educational Change*, eds. Andy Hargreaves et al. (London: Springer, 2010), 555–71; Bruce M. King and Kate Bouchard, "The Capacity to Build Organizational Capacity in Schools," *Journal of Educational Administration* 49, no. 6 (2011): 653–69.

2. Richard Elmore, *Building a New Structure for School Leadership* (Washington, DC: Albert Shanker Institute, 2000), 6.

3. Ibid., 6.

4. King and Bouchard, "Capacity to Build," 657.

5. Ibid., 659.

6. Talbert, "Professional Learning Communities at the Crossroads"; King and Bouchard, "Capacity to Build."

7. James March, "Exploration and Exploitation in Organizational Learning," *Organization Science* 2, no. 1 (1991): 71–87; Charles A. O'Reilly and Michael L. Tushman, "Ambidexterity as a Dynamic Capability: Resolving the Innovator's Dilemma," *Research in Organizational Behavior* 28 (2008): 185–206.

8. O'Reilly and Tushman, "Ambidexterity."

9. Ibid., 187.

10. Meredith Honig, "District Central Office Leadership as Teaching: How Central Office Administrators Support Principals' Development as Instructional Leaders," *Educational Administration Quarterly* 48, no. 4 (2012): 733–74; Michael Knapp et al., *Learning-focused Leadership in Action: Improving Instruction in Schools and Districts* (New York: Routledge, 2014).

11. See Meredith Honig and Lydia Rainey, "Central Office Leadership in Principal Professional Learning Communities: The Practice Beneath the Policy," *Teachers College Record* 116, no. 4 (2014). These researchers studied six principal communities of practice and found significant differences in how central office administrators facilitated principals' conversations. They found that these differences mattered for principal learning. The study did not examine how principal supervisors learned to facilitate these conversations.

12. Ibid., 16.

13. Ibid., 39.

14. Knapp et al., *Learning-Focused Leadership in Action.*

15. Ibid., 200.

16. Vivian Robinson, *Student-Centered Leadership* (San Francisco: John Wiley & Sons, 2011), 47.

17. Karen Miles and Stephen Frank, *The Strategic School: Making the Most of People, Time, and Money* (Thousand Oaks, CA: Corwin Press, 2008) and Viviane Robinson, *Student-Centered Leadership* (San Francisco: Jossey-Bass, 2011), 63.

18. William Johnston, Julia Kaufman, and Lindsey Thompson, "Support for Instructional Leadership," RAND Corporation report, June 2016.

CHAPTER 7

1. Etienne Wenger, *Communities of Practice: Learning, Meaning, and Identity* (Cambridge, UK: Cambridge University Press, 1998).

2. Jean Lave and Etienne Wenger, *Situated learning: Legitimate Peripheral Participation* (Cambridge, UK: Cambridge University Press, 1991).

3. Wenger, *Communities of Practice*, 49.

4. Ibid.

5. Harry F. Wolcott, *The Art of Fieldwork* (Walnut Creek: AltaMira Press, 1995), 246.

6. Ibid.

7. Ibid., 247–48.

8. Paul Cobb et al. "Design Experiments in Educational Research," *Educational Researcher* 32, no. 1 (2003): 9–13; William R. Penuel et al., "Conceptualizing Research–Practice Partnerships as Joint Work at Boundaries," *Journal of Education for Students Placed at Risk* 20, no. 1–2 (2015): 182–97.

9. William R. Penuel et al., "Organizing Research and Development at the Intersection of Learning, Implementation, and Design," *Educational Researcher* 40, no. 7 (2011): 331–37.

10. Erin Henrick, Nicholas Kochmanski, and Paul Cobb, "Practical Measures of Instructional Practice" (paper presented at National Center on Scaling Up Effective Schools, second national conference, Vanderbilt University, Nashville, TN, October 8–9, 2015).

11. Magdalene Lampert, *Teaching Problems and the Problems of Teaching* (New Haven, CT: Yale University Press, 2003).

12. Ibid., 2.

13. Prompts for viewing the video clips were influenced by Project Zero thinking routines (http://www.pz.harvard.edu/thinking-routines).

ACKNOWLEDGMENTS

Writing this book would not have been possible without the help and encouragement of many people. For the initial development of the concept, instructional capacity, I am especially grateful to my husband, Rob, who spent countless hours listening to me talk through the ideas that are at the core of this book. He asked good questions, helped me to sharpen my thinking, and believed in me when I felt most unsure of myself.

I am also incredibly grateful to all of the teachers, principals, district leaders, and professional developers who gave me opportunities to learn from them and with them. Thank you for inviting me into your classrooms, into your staff and principal meetings, into your workshops, and into your intimate conversations with your colleagues. Thank you for making time to answer my questions and for letting me learn alongside you. The practical ideas in this book are rooted in those experiences. Your care and determination to make our schools better for all of our children have made learning from you a great honor and privilege. Your work has inspired me to write this book.

For mentoring me as a researcher and a scholar, I want to thank Pam, Milbrey, Deb, and Joan. I am also grateful to many colleagues and friends who have helped me to try out the ideas in this book with other educators; special thanks go to Terry for being my "sidekick" in piloting these ideas in the early days with school teams, and to Susan and Laura for encouraging me to pursue ways to share these ideas more broadly and for helping me to do so. I am grateful to many other friends who have helped and supported me along the way. Enormous gratitude goes to my friend and colleague Ann, who has encouraged me to pursue these ideas since the very beginning and whose belief in me has had a profound effect on my work. Thanks to Edit and Liam for helping me collect and analyze data that is used in this book. And thank you, Caroline, my editor at HEP, who first encouraged me to submit a book proposal and whose insightful feedback along the way has helped make this book better.

ABOUT THE AUTHOR

Ann Jaquith is the associate director of the Stanford Center for Opportunity Policy in Education (SCOPE), where she works at the intersection of research, practice, and policy. Ann's research focuses on understanding the conditions in educational settings in which instructional improvement occurs. She studies school reform efforts and professional development initiatives. Ann received her doctorate from the Stanford Graduate School of Education.

INDEX

Accelerated Reader, 95
activity triangles, 168–169
adaptation of a resource, 34
administrators. *See* central offices; district administrators; principals
adoption of a resource, 34

boundary objects, 43
boundary spanners and carriers, 43–46
brokering, 43
building instructional capacity
  conducting examinations of practice, 193
  defining a clear learning goal, 193–194
  definition of improvement of teaching and learning, 67
  determining the problem's significance, 192
  focusing on organizational strategy for, 76–84
  generation of more resources, 87–89
  identifying and using all available resources, 194
  identifying problems of practice, 191–192
  organizing for interdependent work, 195
  results of insufficient support at a school (*see* Liberty Middle School)

results of strong support at a school (*see* Cedar Bridge Middle School)
supports for principals (*see* district administrators; leading principal learning)
value in the way resources are used, 195–196

Cedar Bridge Middle School
  addressing an achievement gap, 75–77
  boundary carriers, 44
  collaboration process principles, 103
  community of practice impact, 43
  community of practice use, 25–26, 42
  critiques of the group meeting, 12–13
  decision to establish PLCs, 77–80
  demographic characteristics, 68
  effective use of the PLCs, 83–85, 89
  environment at the school, 11, 13, 69–70, 71, 75, 80
  fitting the PLCs to adult learning needs, 80–81
  generation of more resources, 87–89
  instructional knowledge use, 70–71
  instructional resource inventory, 81–83
  instructional technology use, 17, 18, 71–72, 96

teachers, *continued*
  purpose and design of
    talking-to-the-text, 52–54
  purposeful use of an instructional
    technology, 62–63
  significance of understanding a re-
    source, 54, 56–57, 63–64
  structure of the RA program, 52
  supportive environment example
    (*see* Cedar Bridge Middle
    School)
  unsupportive environment example
    (*see* Liberty Middle School)
Teach for America (TFA), 91, 97, 98
technical challenges for central offices
  identifying goals for principal learn-
    ing, 138
  knowing what principals need to
    know, 137–138
  problem of variation in the content
    of ISVs, 140–141
  problems of implementation of ISVs,
    141–142
  stated goals versus actual results from
    ISVs, 138–139
  what ISVs need to do to work, 139–140
Text Analysis Tool, 72
transformation of a resource, 34